赵洪娟 梅中芳 ◎ 主编

An Introduction to Traditional Chinese Culture in English

中国传统文化英语谈

中国海洋大学出版社
·青岛·

图书在版编目（CIP）数据

中国传统文化英语谈 / 梅中芳, 赵洪娟主编. —青岛：中国海洋大学出版社, 2023.1
ISBN 978-7-5670-3423-5

Ⅰ.①中… Ⅱ.①梅… ②赵… Ⅲ.①中华文化—英文 Ⅳ.①K203

中国国家版本馆 CIP 数据核字（2023）第 008323 号

出版发行	中国海洋大学出版社
社　　址	青岛市香港东路23号　　邮政编码　266071
网　　址	http://pub.ouc.edu.cn
出 版 人	刘文菁
责任编辑	付绍瑜　　　　　　　　电　　话　0532-85902533
电子信箱	184385208@qq.com
策划编辑	邓志科
印　　制	青岛名扬数码印刷有限责任公司
版　　次	2023年1月第1版
印　　次	2023年1月第1次印刷
成品尺寸	170 mm × 230 mm
印　　张	19.25
字　　数	280千
印　　数	1～1000
定　　价	78.00元
订购电话	0532-82032573（传真）

发现印装质量问题，请致电13792806519，由印刷厂负责调换。

编委会

主　编：梅中芳　赵洪娟
副主编：陈　楠　陈宜各　王　娟

前　言

一、编写依据

"国际化"与"跨文化"是英语学科的发展目标。本教材的编写主要基于培养中外交流人才的迫切需要，基于为社会培养具有杰出的外文和中文能力，深入了解中国文化，能充分讲好中国故事、传播好中国声音的优秀人才。《中国传统文化英语谈》一书，旨在帮助学生系统了解中国传统文化的发展脉络和概况，继承和弘扬传统文化精髓，使其能够用英语准确、得体、地道地对外介绍中国传统文化，从而增强、培养学生的人文素养、务实精神、创新意识和家国情怀，推动中外文化交流，向世界展现中国精神。

二、教材特色

课程思政贯彻始终

本教材以党的二十大精神为指导，深度融合课程思政，努力将价值塑造、知识传授和能力培养融为一体，打造课程改革和"金课"建设，实现立德树人的目标。本教材能有效改善中国传统文化失语症现象，教导学生用英语讲好中国故事，让中国传统文化伴随"一带一路"倡议真正"走出去"，不仅可提高学生的跨文化交际能力，更有益于在国际舞台上提升中国文化的软实力。

语言地道、内容丰富

本教材注重输出能力的培养，希望学生用地道的英语准确地讲述中国文化。教材涵盖了中国传统文化核心内容，充分展示了中国文化内涵，挖掘了文化主题背后的核心理念，探寻了中华智慧的精神财富，可帮助学生充实文化储备、领悟文化精髓。教材精选了中国传统文化的中国思想智慧、中国传统节日、中国民俗文化、绘画艺术、丝绸服饰、传统体育、中国饮食、中草药等主题内容。每个主题可体现中国价值观、中国特色及中国精神。教材文章均选自原版外文资料、中国权威书籍或官方网络，力求呈现地道的英语。古今中国人以智慧和心血成就了无数精彩的中国故事，当代中国人更应宣传推广，并以精彩的表达讲好中国故事。

新形态数字教材

本教材提供了各种音视频数字资源、网络素材及慕课资源，教师和学生可通过扫描二维码进行教与学，适合线上、线下、自学等各类教学模式的开展，让授课和知识习得变得轻松愉悦，可让学生更加直观形象地领略中国传统文化魅力。

以学生为中心

本教材以多轮课堂教学实践为基础，吸取国内同类教材优点，以学生为中心，从难易度、趣味性、实践性等各方面对教材文章进行了精心选择。考虑到学生的认知特点、学习能力、兴趣爱好等因素，"因地制宜""因人制宜"，形成了极具特色并适合普通高校大学生水平、符合学科要求的中国传统文化教程。教材中选取各类英语考试真题及练习题，如全国大学生英语竞赛试题，全国大学生四六级考试真题，全国高校英语专业四级、八级考试真题，题型多样，适合各级本科生、研究生及英语爱好者用以提升英语能力。

三、教材体系和结构

本教材共包括十二个单元，分为十二个主题。每个单元分别根据主题提供听、说、读、写、译的练习。

单元主要结构如下：

Lead-in 部分为话题导入，设计了相关的话题讨论或小练习，旨在引起学生兴趣，进行头脑风暴。

Reading 部分包括两三篇阅读篇章，设计为精读部分，旨在培养学生的阅读能力，提高学生的词汇量及理解力。

Listening and Speaking 部分涵盖两三篇对话或短文，含音频及视频资料，旨在提高学生的听力理解水平及口语表达能力。

Viewing 部分即本单元主题部分的升华，实则是课程思政的融合，旨在提高学生的文化修养，实现立德树人的目标。

Practising 部分集中了翻译、作文、完形填空等各类题型，主要培养学生的写作与翻译能力。此外，本教材还配备了慕课、课件、参考网站等教学资源，供教师参阅。

有些单元附加了 Further Reading 及 Appreciation，为本专题内容的知识补充及美文赏析，旨在提高学生的泛读能力，开阔视野。

本教材既适用于中国普通高校非英语专业本科生的大学英语及选修课程，也可作为英语专业及研究生低年级的选修课程，还可供来华旅游或留学的学生以及对中国传统文化感兴趣的外国友人使用。

四、编写团队

本教材的编写团队由一线授课教师组成，主要负责英语专业研究生及本科生教学、大学英语教学及学校各文化类课程教学。教材凝聚了他们的经验、智慧及创新。同时，出版社的多位老师进行了多次审稿、修改，其严格的把关、校对提高了本教材的质量，在此真诚地表示感谢。由于编者水平有限，期待各位专家和师生批评指正。

另特别感谢本书的图片提供者：青岛科技大学艺术学院禹青教授；青岛市手工艺协会刘桂燕；青岛科技大学融媒体中心；山东省非物质文化遗产葫芦书法微烙传承人王向阳、王建忠；青岛科技大学国画专业2018级本科生薛增辉。

编　者

2022年11月

CONTENTS

Unit 1　Traditional Chinese Festivals ·· 001

Unit 2　Confucian Thoughts　·· 036

Unit 3　Laozi's Philosophy ·· 067

Unit 4　Chinese Painting ·· 082

Unit 5　Chinese Opera ·· 111

Unit 6　Traditional Chinese Handicrafts ··· 138

Unit 7　Chinese Embroidery ··· 168

Unit 8　Chinese Kung Fu ·· 188

Unit 9　Chinese Tea Culture ··· 205

Unit 10　Chinese Cuisine ·· 222

Unit 11　Dunhuang Frescoes ·· 247

Unit 12　Traditional Chinese Medicine ··· 268

References and Websites ··· 287

Traditional Chinese Festivals

Learning Objectives

After learning this unit, you will be able to:
- know about Chinese calendar;
- learn the basic information about some traditional Chinese festivals, including words and expressions, proper names, etc;
- try to introduce some important Chinese festivals in English;
- trace sources of Chinese festivals.

China's traditional festivals are diverse in forms and rich in content and are an integral part of the long history and culture of the Chinese nation. Traditional festivals are important carriers of national culture. During the long process of historical development, a host of excellent cultural elements of the Chinese country have become integrated, which are a great spiritual wealth for the whole country, and exert positive effects in shaping national identity and cultivating national spirit.

Traditional festivals not only help people to increase their knowledge and gain enlightenment, but also contribute to promoting virtues, cultivating noble sentiments, and advancing traditions. They also play an important role in enhancing national cohesion, maintaining social harmony and stability, elevating the soft power of the country, and strengthening the competitiveness of the country. In order to protect traditional festivals, China adjusted the national statutory holidays in 2007, listing the Qingming Festival, the Dragon Boat Festival, and the Mid-Autumn Festival as statutory holidays alongside the Spring Festival. In addition, China is also strengthening the protection of intangible cultural heritage, including festivals. Traditional festivals have been added to the list of intangible cultural heritage at all levels.

Part I Lead-in

Solar Terms

Match the following solar terms with the right translation.

处暑	Grain in Ear
立秋	Winter Solstice
惊蛰	End of Heat
小满	Major Heat
冬至	Beginning of Autumn
春分	Frost's Descent
小寒	Waking of Insects
霜降	Vernal Equinox
芒种	Minor Cold
大暑	Grain Buds

Listen to the passage and fill in the blanks with the exact words or phrases you hear.

The 24 solar terms, a system considered to be China's fifth great invention, were added to the world's intangible cultural heritage list in November, 2016. The system _____ people's observations of the sun's motion throughout the year and its influence on climate, mostly carried out on the lower reaches of the Yellow River where Chinese civilization was born. The system was completely established during the Qin and Han dynasties. It was crucial to _____ such as when to sow seeds and when to harvest. Today, it is still of great help for people to better prepare their bodies for the changes of climate.

As the first solar term, Beginning of Spring lifts the curtain of spring. When Beginning of Spring arrives, days get longer and sunlight gets warmer. Temperature, the length of sunlight and the amount of rainfall are all at the turning points of the year. Similar to crops, human bodies also start a new round of growth from this day. People should open the windows _____ to allow the air to circulate and take more physical exercises to enhance their immunity. An old Chinese saying goes like this, "Spring begins and rain arrive. Get up early and sleep late." It is to remind the farmers that the annual farming is about to begin.

It is believed that if someone can make an egg stand on the day of Start of Spring, he will _____ in the future. According to astronomers and physicists, setting an egg upright has nothing to do with time, but with mechanics.

Spring is also the best season for kite-flying. As a traditional Chinese folk activity, it has a history of more than 2,000 years. It can help build one's health and prevent diseases. It also has the effect of promoting blood circulation and _____ metabolism.

Part II Reading

Chinese Calendar

Gregorian calendar 公历；阳历

zodiac [ˈzəʊdiæk] n. 黄道带；星座；〈罕〉一圈

astrology [əˈstrɒlədʒi] n. 占星术；占星学

The Chinese calendar has 12 or 13 lunar months per year, and is about 20 to 50 days behind the **Gregorian calendar**. It's used to determine the dates of traditional Chinese festivals, like Chinese New Year and Mid-Autumn. It's also used for Chinese **zodiac astrology**, and many Chinese still celebrate their Chinese calendar birthdays.

What is Chinese Lunar Calendar and How it Works?

The Chinese calendar is also called the lunar calendar, Yin calendar or Xia calendar in China. The Chinese calendar is based on the orbits of the moon and earth. When the moon moves into a line with the earth and the sun, it comes the first day of the lunar month. When the moon is full, it comes the middle of the month. So there are 29 or 30 days in a month. There are 12 or 13 months in a lunar year. For 12 months, there will be 354 or 355 days in a year. To **compensate** the other 10 days with the Gregorian calendar, there is **a leap month** for about 2 or 3 lunar years.

In ancient China, the Chinese calendar was used to choose the dates for farming, weddings, and building and moving into new houses. Nowadays, most Chinese people use the Gregorian calendar for their daily life arrangements. But most Chinese still care about lunar dates because traditional festivals are based on the lunar calendar.

compensate ['kɒmpenseɪt] v. 补偿；弥补；抵消

Chinese Calendar Days

Ancient Chinese people used the 12 heavenly systems and 10 earthly branches to name each hour of a day. The Western hour-minute-second system was brought into China in the Qing dynasty (1644—1911). On a Chinese calendar, all dates use a regular two characters.

Days 1 to 10 of a month are written with Chinese number characters and **preceded** by the Chinese character 初 (which means "beginning" or "first"). For example, the 10th of the month is 初十. Days 11 to 20 are written as regular two-character Chinese numerals. For example, 十五

precede [prɪ'siːd] v. 在……之前发生或出现，先于

is the 15th day of the month, and 二十 is the 20th. Days 21 to 29 are written with the character 廿 (which means "20") preceding the characters "one" through "nine". For example, 廿三 is the 23rd day of the month. Day 30 is written as 30 usually is in Chinese 三十.

Chinese Calendar Months

The length of a Chinese calendar month is not fixed from year to year. There are 29 days in a short month, which is also called a "small month" in Chinese, while there are 30 days in a long month, called a "big month". In this way, a 12-month lunar year (with six 29-day months and six 30-day months) has only 354 days.

To keep the lunar calendar in **synch** with solar cycles (which thereby compensates for lost days compared to the Gregorian calendar), there is a **leap month** every two or three lunar years.

Leap Months—When Chinese Add a 13th Month

As a lunar month is on average 0.92 days shorter than a "solar month", the lunar calendar is just under a day per month slower than the solar calendar.

To prevent the lunar calendar from becoming more than half a month of sync with the solar calendar, an extra "leap month" is added in the Chinese calendar every 32 or 33 months. So every second or third Chinese calendar year has 13 months and 383 to 385 days.

The last Chinese calendar leap month was in 2020. There were two fourth lunar months: month 4 and then "**intercalary** month 4"—the leap month.

The next leap month will be in 2023, when a second

---

synch [sɪŋk] *n.* 同时，同步

leap month 闰月

intercalary [ɪnˈtɜːkələrɪ] *adj.* 插在中间的，被夹于中间的

lunar month 2 will be observed.

Names of Chinese Lunar Months

Ancient Chinese people named each lunar month according to what they or nature traditionally did in that month. See below:

Month	Chinese	English	Explanation
1	正月	Start Month	It starts the year
2	杏月	Apricot Month	Apricot trees blossom
3	桃月	Peach Month	Peach trees blossom
4	槐月	Locust Tree Month	Locust trees blossom
5	蒲月	Sweet Sedge Month	Lunar month 5 day 5 is the Dragon Boat Festival
6	荷月	Lotus Month	Lotus flowers bloom
7	巧月	Skill Month	On lunar month 7 day 7, Chinese Valentine's Day
8	桂月	Osmanthus Month	Osmanthus flowers bloom
9	菊月	Chrysanthemum Month	Chrysanthemum flowers bloom
10	阳月	Yang Month	The Taoist *yang* force is believed to be strong this month
11	冬月	Winter Month	The winter solstice is in this month
12	腊月	Preserved Month	Chinese preserve meats ready for Spring Festival

Chinese Calendar VS Gregorian Calendar

A Chinese calendar is based on the movement of the moon. When the moon moves into a line with the earth and the sun, the new lunar month begins. When the moon is full, it is the middle of the month. The circle is about 29 days. The lunar month has 29 or 30 days for a month. Gregorian calendar is calculated by the movement of sun, which has 30 or 31 days for a month. There is 21 to 51 days behind the corresponding Gregorian calendar date (intercalary months excepted).

How People Use Chinese Calendar

Chinese people use the lunar calendar to define the Chinese traditional festivals, 24 solar terms and choose a lucky day for wedding, building or moving into new house and so on.

Traditional Chinese Festivals

Festivals are important to Chinese people. All traditional Chinese festivals are based on the lunar calendar. The Spring Festival is on the first day of the lunar year and the Dragon Boat Festival is on the fifth day of the fifth month. Mid-Autumn Festival is on the 15th day of the 8th lunar month. Qixi Festival ("Double-Seventh" or "Chinese Valentine's Day") is on day 7 of lunar month 7.

If you want to know the date of a traditional Chinese festival, then you must know its lunar calendar date before looking it up for a particular year.

Chinese Zodiac Animals

The Chinese zodiac year is (popularly) based on the lunar calendar. A zodiac year is from the first day to the last day of a lunar year, starting/ending at some point in January/February of the Gregorian calendar. For example, 2022 was the year of Tiger, which was from Feb. 01, 2022 to Jan. 21, 2023.

There are twelve animals in the Chinese zodiac: Rat (Mouse), Ox (Bull), Tiger, Rabbit, Dragon, Snake, Horse, Goat, Monkey, Rooster (Cock), Dog, and Pig. The twelve animals are always in this order in the cycle and each one represents a year. If you want to find out your zodiac animal, then check your birthday according to a Chinese calendar, especially if you were born in January/February.

Auspicious Days, Months, and Years in China

Chinese people use the lunar calendar to choose a good date for important events such as weddings or commencement of building a house. Some dates on a Chinese calendar are considered not good for weddings or moving house, while there are other days that are recommended for doing certain things.

The 3rd and 17th days of each lunar month are considered unlucky days.

Auspicious days are chosen by some fortune tellers, particularly in countryside areas of China. When choosing the date for getting married, the bride and groom each **submit** their time, date, month, and year of birth to a fortune teller who calculates the best date for getting married. This is called the matching of astrological birth data known as 生辰八字 (shengchen bazi).

The 24 Solar Terms

In the traditional Chinese solar calendar, a year was divided into 24 parts, each of 15 or 16 days, called the 24 solar terms, which were defined by the sun's position relative to the earth.

In ancient China, people used the 24 solar terms to define the four seasons and determine the right time to grow crops and harvest them. For example, the first solar term is called Li Chun, which means "Beginning of Spring". It is the time for planting rice in south China.

There were originally only four solar terms in the

Shang dynasty: the summer solstice, the winter solstice and the spring and autumn equinoxes. During the Han dynasty, however, the solar year was further split into 24 solar terms known as 节气. These solar terms mark particular **astronomical** events such as equinoxes, solstices and other natural occurrences such as weather changes to guide farmers. The 24 solar terms are as follows:

astronomical
[ˌæstrəˈnɒmɪkl]
adj. 天文学的

立春	Beginning of Spring	立秋	Beginning of Autumn
雨水	Rainwater	处暑	End of Heat
惊蛰	Waking of Insects	白露	White Dew
春分	Vernal Equinox	秋分	Autumn Equinox
清明	Pure Brightness	寒露	Cold Dew
谷雨	Grain Rain	霜降	Frost's Descent
立夏	Beginning of Summer	立冬	Beginning of Winter
小满	Grain Buds	小雪	Minor Snow
芒种	Grain in Ear	大雪	Major Snow
夏至	Summer Solstice	冬至	Winter Solstice
小暑	Minor Heat	小寒	Minor Cold
大暑	Major Heat	大寒	Major Cold

Naming the Years and the 60-Year Cycle

Chinese use the 10 Heavenly Stems and 12 Earthly Branches to name the years.

The 10 Heavenly Stems are 甲 (Jia), 乙 (Yi), 丙 (Bing), 丁 (Ding), 戊 (Wu), 己 (Ji), 庚 (Geng), 辛 (Xin), 壬 (Ren), and 癸 (Gui).

The 12 Earthly Branches are 子 (Zi), 丑 (Chou), 寅 (Yin), 卯 (Mao), 辰 (Chen), 巳 (Si), 午 (Wu), 未 (Wei), 申 (Shen), 酉 (You), 戌 (Xu), and 亥 (Hai).

For example, the year 2021 is called 辛丑 (Stem 8 Branch 2) and the year 2022 is called 壬寅 (Stem 9 Branch 3).

When a new lunar year comes, the heavenly stem and earthly branch each move on to the next one and combine to form the year's name—always an odd (*yang*) stem with an odd (*yang*) branch or even (*yin*) stem with even (*yin*) branch. And so, the 10 heavenly stems and 12 earthly branches combine in a 60-year cycle (the 30 *yang* combinations **interposed** with the 30 *yin* combinations).

interpose
[ˌɪntəˈpəʊz] *vt.*
插(话);插入;
打断

The Five Elements

In ancient China, people believed that all things in the world were composed of five elements, which were called Metal, Wood, Water, Fire, and Earth. Each element was associated with a 12-year zodiac cycle, producing another 60-year cycle to parallel the Heavenly Stems and Earthly Branches year system.

Many Chinese use their birth date to find out the element they belong to as well as their zodiac sign to predict their luck in marriage, career development, or business success.

The History of the Chinese Lunar Calendar

Existing possibly for 4,000 years in some form, the uncertain early history of the Chinese lunar calendar can be traced back to **questionable** Zhou dynasty writings about the Xia dynasty (2070 BC-1600 BC). So, the Chinese calendar is also called the Xia calendar.

However, the Chinese lunar calendar was not definitely known to have been developed until the Spring and Autumn Period (770 BC-476 BC) of the Zhou era, whose preserved Confucian classics recorded its use.

The **succeeding** dynasties continued to use the lunar calendar and made some small changes from time to time. The lunar calendar was called the Taichu calendar during Han dynasty (206 BC-220 AD) and Huangji Calendar in Tang dynasty (618-907). Other Asian countries with cultural links to China, such as Korea, Vietnam, and Japan used the Huangji Calendar of the Tang dynasty until modern times.

The Gregorian calendar is also the official calendar in China and used for all public and business affairs. This includes holidays such as Labor Day, Women's Day, Chinese National Day, and the international New Year. However, the Chinese calendar still plays an important and dominant role in everyday life. It is used to govern traditional Chinese holidays such as the Lantern Festival, Tomb-Sweeping Day (or Qingming Festival), Mid-Autumn Festival, and, of course, the Chinese New Year.

---

questionable
['kwestʃənəbl]
adj. 可疑的，有疑问的

succeeding
[sək'si:dɪŋ] adj.
以后的，随后的

Reading Comprehension.

Read the passage and decide whether the following statements are true (T) or false (F).

1. The Chinese calendar is based on the orbits of the sun and earth. _____
2. There are 12 or 13 months in a lunar year. _____
3. Since the Qing dynasty, China started to use hour-minute-second system. _____
4. There are 29 days in a "small month" in Chinese. _____
5. Every second or third Chinese calendar year has 13 months. _____
6. Ancient Chinese people named 10th lunar month "Ju Month" for Chrysanthemum flowers bloom in this month. _____
7. During the Han dynasty, 24 solar terms come into being. _____
8. The 10 heavenly stems and 12 earthly branches combine in a 60-year cycle. _____
9. All things in the world were composed of five elements in modern society of China. _____
10. The earliest Chinese lunar calendar was recorded in the Confucian classics. _____

More Than Just Moon Cakes: A Guide to Mid-Autumn Festival

rip [rip] *v.* 撕，扯
pomelo ['pɒmələu] *n.* 柚子
sample ['sɑːmpl] *v.* 尝，尝试（食品、饮料）

It's time to hang a lantern, **rip** open a moon cake and peel a **pomelo**—Mid-Autumn Festival is here.

Falling on the 15th day of the eighth lunar month, Mid-Autumn Festival, or Moon Festival, is when families gather to **sample** autumn harvests, light lanterns and admire what's believed to be the fullest moon of the year.

The event—is celebrated primarily in East and Southeast Asia. Mid-Autumn Festival became an official celebration in China during the Tang dynasty (618–907), still there isn't one single answer to the question of when and how the Mid-Autumn Festival began. Many believe the **fete** was first mentioned in the ***Book of Rites***①, a Confucius classic on **bureaucracy** and **rituals** written more than 2,400 years ago. It was described as a day for emperors to celebrate the year's harvest by giving offerings to the moon and hosting a great feast.

Today, the Mid-Autumn Festival is an **incredibly** important family gathering—it's when "people and the moon reunite to form a full circle", as an old saying goes.

Like many cultural celebrations, the Mid-Autumn Festival is **shrouded** in myth. One of the most beloved—and **tragic**—pieces of **folklore** tells the story of how Chang'e became the moon goddess.

According to the legend, after mythological Chinese **archer** Hou Yi **courageously** shot down nine surplus suns—leaving only one, in effect protecting the world from being **scorched** completely—he was given an **elixir** from heaven. Hou Yi's wife Chang'e drank the elixir while protecting it from a greedy **apprentice**, but became so light that she **floated** to the moon. Missing his wife, Hou Yi prepared a feast every year on the day when the moon was at its fullest, hoping to get a **glimpse** of his wife's shadow.

Just how well-known is this story? China's spacecraft, Chang'e 1, 2, 3 and 4, were named in honor of Chang'e. Yutu (Jade Rabbit)—China's moon **rover**—was named after the legendary rabbit that was sent to accompany Chang'e to the moon.

When it comes to the festival, customs vary throughout Asia. The Mid-Autumn Festival is considered "children's day" in Vietnam and celebrations include paper lantern fairs and lion dance **parades**. Meanwhile, in southern China, most people will light a lantern and eat autumn fruits such as pomelo and starfruit. Some villages in Hong Kong still **preserve** the tradition of fire dragon dancing through a narrow **alley**.

One of the biggest stars of the Mid-Autumn Festival is the moon cake—it's as important to festivities as turkey is to Thanksgiving and **latkes**② are to **Hanukkah**③. The calorie-packed pastry is sliced up and shared like a cake between families and friends. The most common moon cake is made of lotus seed paste, salted egg yolk and **lard**—which explains why a palm-sized cake can contain about 1,000 calories. Nuts, red beans and **custards** are some other popular **ingredients**.

In recent years, big **brands** have taken to creating specially designed moon cakes. The Palace Museum in Beijing offers some particularly **stunning** ones. Bakery brands have also come up with modern variations—ice cream coated in chocolate, for example—that offer **alternatives** to those who aren't fond of traditional moon cakes.

brand [brænd] n. 品牌；一种；类型
stunning ['stʌnɪŋ] adj. 极好的，令人震惊的
alternative [ɔːl'tɜːnətɪv] n. 可供选择的事物

Notes:

① *Book of Rites*：《礼记》，是中国古代一部重要的典章制度选集，共二十卷四十九篇，书中内容主要写先秦的礼制，是研究先秦社会的重要资料，是一部儒家思想的资料汇编。

② Latke：炸土豆饼，光明节的传统食物之一。

③ Hanukkah: ['hænʊkə] 光明节，历时八天的犹太人节日。

Reading Comprehension.

Choose the best answer according to the text.

1. What are not the special foods in the Mid-Autumn Festival? _____
   A. Starfruit.　　　　　　　　　B. Custard.
   C. Calorie-Packed Pastry.　　　D. Pomelo.

2. Which kind of celebration is not held in China? _____
   A. It is considered as "Children's Day".
   B. To hang a lantern.
   C. Fire dragon dancing.
   D. To have some fruit to eat, such as a pomelo.

3. What are not the origins of the Mid-Autumn Festival? _____
   A. People should give offerings to the moon.
   B. It possibly began in Tang dynasty.
   C. It is used to celebrate the year's harvest.
   D. Emperors pray to the moon.

4. According to the legend of the Mid-Autumn Festival, what is true in the following statements? _____

   A. Chang'e floated to the moon in order to protect the greedy apprentice.

   B. When the moon was full, Hou Yi hoped to see his wife.

   C. It is Hou Yi who drank the elixir given from heaven.

   D. China's moon rover—Yutu, was sent to accompany Chang'e.

5. What is the theme of the Mid-Autumn Festival? _____

   A. Family reunion.

   B. China's unity.

   C. Love to the motherland.

   D. Integrity.

Work in groups to discuss the following questions.

- Could you tell the story of "Chang E's Flight to the Moon"?
- Why is the Mid-Autumn Festival a festival of family reunions?
- Do you know some other traditional Chinese festivals of family reunion?
- What is the origin of the custom of eating moon cakes?
- Could you recite some Chinese classic poetry on the moon? And try to translate them.

Dragon Boat Festival

[A] Dragon Boat Festival, also called Duanwu Festival, is one of the four grandest **traditional festivals** in China, falling on the 5th day of the 5th month in Chinese **lunar calendar**. The other three are Chinese New Year, Mid-Autumn Festival and Qingming Festival.

[B] Time for Dragon Boat Race

People enjoy a 3-day holiday for celebrations, among which the dragon boat race is the most popular. The **iconic** festival food is Zongzi (sticky rice dumplings).

[C] A Day to Commemorate Qu Yuan & Ward Off Bad Things

It has been **observed** for over 2,000 years in China, to

traditional festivals 传统节日

lunar calendar 农历

iconic [aɪˈkɒnɪk] *adj.* 符号的；图标的；图符的

observe [əbˈzɜːv] *v.* 观察；看到；评论；遵守；庆祝

patriotic [ˌpætrɪˈɒtɪk]
adj. 爱国的，有爱国心的
calamus [ˈkæləməs]
n. 省藤属植物，菖蒲，羽根
wormwood [ˈwɜːmwʊd]
n. 蒿草
pouches [paʊtʃɪz]
n. 香囊

commemorate Qu Yuan (340 BC−278 BC), an ancient Chinese **patriotic** poet. It is also a day to ward off evil spirits, diseases, pests and other poisonous animals by hanging **calamus** and **wormwood**, wearing perfume **pouches**, drinking realgar wine, bathing in herbal water, etc.

[D] When is Dragon Boat Festival?

Chinese Dragon Boat Festival is on the 5th day of the 5th lunar month. In Gregorian calendar, it varies every year, generally falling in June and in a very few years in late May. The dragon boat holiday in China is three days long. In 2021, the festival date was June 14 and the holiday lasts from June 12 to 14. In 2022, it falls on June 3 and the holiday is from June 3 to 5.

Year	Date	Holiday
2020	June 25	June 25-27
2021	June 14	June 12-14
2022	June 3	June 3-5
2023	June 22	June 22-24
2024	June 10	June 8-10
2025	May 31	May 31-June 2

[E] What is Dragon Boat Festival for?

★Commemorating Qu Yuan

Why is the Dragon Boat Festival celebrated? The earliest origin of the Chinese Dragon Boat Festival can be dated to "dragon worship" in Prehistoric Times (1.7 million years ago−2100 BC), while the most popular origin is closely related to the great poet Qu

Yuan in the Warring States Period (475BC−221BC).

[F] Qu Yuan was a minister in his home State of Chu, who wrote a lot of poems and proposed many reforms to show his care and devotion to his country. After the reform failed and he was **exiled** by the king, he chose to drown himself on the fifth day of the fifth lunar month in the river rather than seeing his country **invaded** and conquered by the State of Qin. After he **drowned** himself, people rowed boats to save him but failed. Since then, people commemorate Qu Yuan on the 5th day of the 5th lunar month every year, by rowing a boat to feed fish with Zongzi, so that they would not give a bite on Qu Yuan's body.

[G] Great people like Wu Zixu and Cao E also died on the same day, so in certain areas, people also commemorate them during the festival.

★Easing Diseases, Preventing Epidemics and Warding off Evil Spirits

[H] Why is the Dragon Boat Festival so important? In addition to its memorial meaning, there is some actual use. Originally, the festival was set close to Summer **Solstice**, when pests, other poisonous animals and germs start to become more active. Hence, people took measures to prevent the diseases and epidemics from happening on that day and later evil spirits were also added to the list to be prevented. Many of the customs have been handed down till today.

[I] How to Celebrate Dragon Boat Festival-Top Activities & Customs?

exile [ˈeksaɪl] v. 流放，放逐

invade [ɪnˈveɪd] v. 涌入；侵袭；侵犯；干扰

drown [draʊn] v. （使）淹死；盖过，淹没

solstice [ˈsɒlstɪs] n. 至，至日

1. Dragon Boat Racing

Dragon boats are thus named because the fore and **stern** of the boat are in the shape of the traditional Chinese dragon. A team of people works the oars in a bid to reach the **destination** before other teams. One team member sits at the front of the boat beating a drum in order to maintain **morale** and ensure that the rowers keep in time with one another. Now it has turned out to be a sport event not only held in China, but also observed in Japan, Vietnam, USA, Canada and UK, etc.

[J] ### 2. Eating Zongzi

Zongzi is a pyramid-shaped **glutinous** rice dumpling wrapped in **reed** leaves. It has various fillings. In northern China, people favor the **jujubes** as the filling, while the south sweetened bean paste, fresh meat, or egg yolk. Nowadays, Zongzi already becomes a typical food, which can be easily found in supermarkets and food stores. However, some families still **retain** the tradition of making Zongzi on the festival day.

[K] 3. Hanging **Calamus** and **Wormwood**

It is said that hanging wormwood leaves on the door can protect people living inside from diseases. Calamus leaves look like swords; they are hung to ward off evil spirits. From a scientific point of view, the Dragon Boat Festival falls in the hot summer, which **breeds germs** easily and pests and other poisonous animals are active; both wormwood and calamus give off special fragrance, which can clean the air and drive out mosquitoes and insects, thus help people staying away from diseases and epidemics.

[L] 4. Wearing Perfume Pouches

This custom has the same purpose as hanging calamus and wormwood, as the pouches are always filled with Chinese herbal medicines which can **repel** pests and other poisonous animals. Nowadays, it is more popular among children and the pouches are made into various shapes, including the traditional Zongzi pattern, various animals, **gourd**, pumpkin and flowers.

[M] 5. Pasting Portrait of Zhong Kui

Zhong Kui was a very ugly immortal who was responsible for driving out evil spirits. At the festival, people paste his portrait on the door or hang it in the room to protect their house.

[N] Besides, there are some customs popular in certain areas, including tiring five-color silk necklace, bracelet, and anklet; drinking **realgar wine**; bathing with herbal water; bathing in the water where a

fetch [fetʃ] *v.* 去拿；卖得；售得；去取

dragon boat race was held; **fetching** water at noon; and picking up herbal medicines.

Reading Comprehension.

In this section, you are going to read a passage with ten statements attached to it. Each statement contains information given in one of the paragraphs. Identify the paragraph from which the information is derived. You may choose a paragraph more than once. Each paragraph is marked with a letter.

1. The Chinese Dragon Boat Festival can be traced back to Prehistoric Times. _____

2. In 2023, the date of the Duanwu Festival is June 22. _____

3. The traditional Zongzi pattern filled with Chinese herbal medicines is popular nowadays. _____

4. In hot summer, pests and other poisonous animals are active. _____

5. People paste the portrait on the door, which could protect their house. _____

6. Lantern Festival is not one of the four grandest traditional festivals in China. _____

7. Many of the customs have been passed down to now. _____

8. Dragon Boat Festival is celebrated to commemorate Qu Yuan. _____

9. Special fragrances of some plants can clean the air. _____

10. Qu Yuan proposed many reforms, but failed and was exiled. _____

Answer the following questions according to the text.

- When do Chinese people celebrate the Dragon Boat Festival every year?
- Why did Qu Yuan commit suicide?
- How do people celebrate the Dragon Boat Festival now?
- Why do parents prepare perfume pouches for their children on the Dragon Boat Festival?

Work in groups to discuss the following questions.

- Do you know about the four grandest festivals in China? Try to introduce them in English.
- Try to tell some stories and legends about the four traditional grand festivals.

Part III Listening and Speaking

Lantern Festival

New Words

carnival	[ˈkɑːnɪvl]	n.	狂欢节；嘉年华
inheritor	[ɪnˈherɪtə(r)]	n.	继承人，后继者
customary	[ˈkʌstəməri]	adj.	习俗的，习惯的
signature	[ˈsɪɡnətʃə]	n.	签名，标识；鲜明特色
representative	[ˌreprɪˈzentətɪv]	n.	代表；继任者
glitter	[ˈɡlɪtə(r)]	vi.	闪烁，闪耀
inscribe	[ɪnˈskraɪb]	vt.	雕，刻；题写，题献
delicacy	[ˈdelɪkəsi]	n.	佳肴；精美
translucent	[trænzˈluːsnt]	adj.	半透明的；透亮的
bid	[bɪd]	v.	努力争取；问候，道别

Proper Name

intangible cultural heritage	非物质文化遗产

Listening Comprehension.

In this section, you will hear an introduction to the Chinese Lantern Festival. Try to understand it and finish the following questions.

1. Which is not included in the celebrations of Lantern Festival? _____
   A. Lantern show.   B. Ice sculptures.
   C. Eating tangyuan.   D. Eating fish.

2. The Qinhuai Lantern Show can date back more than _____ years.
   A. 50   B. 170
   C. 500   D. 1,700

3. _____ is inscribed as one of China's first national intangible cultural heritages.
   A. Qinhuai Lantern show   B. Zigong Lantern Show
   C. Yuyuan Lantern Show   D. Beijing Lantern Show

4. To date, New Zealand has successfully hosted _____ Lantern Festival shows.

   A. 47
   B. 20
   C. 40
   D. 8

5. Which is not included in the sweet fillings of tangyuan?

   A. Sesame.
   B. Savory.
   C. Meat or vegetables.
   D. Jujube paste.

Listen again and decide whether the following statements are true (T) or false (F).

1. Lantern Festival marks the end of Spring Festival celebrations. _____
2. Zigong Lantern Show and Yuyuan Lantern Show are held annually during Lantern Festival and run for more than 50 days. _____
3. It was Gu Yeliang who sent the art of Qinhuai lanterns to foreign countries. _____
4. Lanterns with lit candles are signatures of the south. _____
5. Sometimes tangyuan will be stuffed in a coin to symbolize the wholesomeness of a family. _____
6. Lantern Festival is a festival to say goodbye to their families. _____

Work in groups to discuss the following questions.

- What are the customs of the Lantern Festival?
- What are the regional differences in China's lantern art culture?
- What do you know about China's national intangible cultural heritage? Could you introduce some in your hometown?

Qingming Festival

New Words		
deceased	[dɪˈsiːst]	a. 已故的
statutory	[ˈstætʃətri]	a. 法定的
glutinous	[ˈgluːtənəs]	a. 黏的
Proper Name		
pay tribute to ancestors		缅怀先人
spring-outing		踏青
tomb sweeping		扫墓
statutory holiday		法定节假日

Listening Comprehension.

Listen to the following passage and fill in the blanks with the exact words you hear.

The Qingming Festival, or Tomb Sweeping Day, is a traditional Chinese festival that (1) _____ back more than 2,500 years. It falls on the first day of the fifth solar term of the year and usually varies from April 4 to 6. As the name implies, the holiday was (2) _____ a time when the admiration for life mixed with the sorrow of death. It is when the county pays tribute to deceased family members and worships (3) _____.

How do Chinese people celebrate the festival?

Tomb Sweeping

The most central tradition of the Qingming Festival is tomb sweeping. People visit their ancestors' graves, offering flowers and food, (4) _____ weeds of burning joss paper to show their respect. As (5) _____ of environmental protection increases, people have turned to more eco-friendly ways and even hold (6) _____ ceremonies instead.

Eating Cold Food

Qingming follows the Hanshi Festival which (7) _____ to the tradition of eating cold food on this day. Qingtuan, made of glutinous rice and red beans, is among the most popular. In some areas, people also eat (8) _____ eggs, cold pancakes or Sanzi.

Spring Outing

Qingming Festival is usually a time of warmer weather and blossoming flowers. After China set a three-day statutory holiday beginning in 2009, more people chose outdoor activities or short-distance trips amid the holiday, which (9) _____ domestic tourisms. In 2020, the total number of domestic tourists during holidays reached 43 million, a year-on-year decrease of 61%. With the (10) _____ under control, the number this year is expected to surge. This year's Qingming Festival falls on April 4, the same day as Easter.

Appreciation.

The Mourning Day
By Du Mu (803–852)
A drizzling rain falls like tears on the Mourning Day;
The mourner's heart is going to break on his way.
Where can a wine shop be found to drown his sad hours?
A cowherd points to a cot mid apricot flowers.

——许渊冲译

Listening Comprehension.

Watch a short video of the **Qixi Festival** *and decide whether the following statements are true (T) or false (F).*

1. China's Valentine's Day, Qixi is celebrated on the seventh day in July. _____

2. Qixi carries the symbolic meaning that you will choose your own love and remain faithful for life. _____

3. Lovebirds no longer have difficulties in reuniting with the help of high-speed railways in modern times. _____

4. Qixi Festival was created in memory of two ancient lovers who were separated by the Jade Emperor and only allowed to meet once a year. _____

5. Times have changed the role of women in China. They will pursue their love

courageously and no longer be bound to domestic life like the Weaver Girl.

Fill in the blanks. The first letters have been given.

In China, the lovers' festival is the Qixi Festival, celebrated on the seventh day of the seventh l _____ month which is often in August based on the s _____ calendar. So it is also called the Double S _____ Festival or Qiqiao Festival. It commemorates the day when the cowherd and the weaver girl meet on a bridge of m _____ across the M _____ Way. Unlike what Western people often do on St. Valentine's Day, Chinese people don't put much e _____ on giving chocolates, flowers and kisses. Instead, in the evening, people sit o _____ to look up into the the s _____ sky. And people usually prepare tea, wine, fruits, peanuts, dates, flowers and incense as o _____ to the weaver girl, and p _____ for good luck, love, health and a happy family.

Work in groups to discuss the following questions.

- What do you think of the translation for 七夕节?
- Could you tell "the legend of the Weaver Girl and the Cowherd" in English?
- How is Qixi Festival Celebrated in China?
- What is true love?

Part IV Viewing

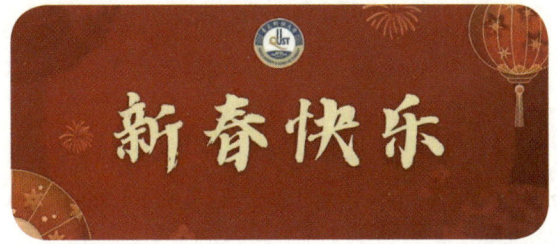

Watch a short video of the **Spring Festival** and discuss the following questions in English.

- How to celebrate Spring Festival in China?
- What are the origins of these customs?
- What are any development and changes for Chinese people to celebrate Spring Festival?
- What are the cultural connotations of the Spring Festival?
- Should the Chinese character "fu"（福）be pasted upside down?
- Do you know the legends related with Spring Festival? (Monster Nian; Door Gods, etc.)

Appreciation.

New Year's Day

Wang Anshi (Song dynasty)

Amid the boom of firecrackers a year has come to an end,

And the spring wind has wafted warm breath to the wine.

While the rising sun shines over each and every household,

People would put up new peachwood charm for the old.

 Part V Practising

Dictation.

Listen to the following passage. Altogether the passage will be read to you four times. During the first reading, which will be done at normal speed, listen and try to understand the  meaning. For the second and third readings, the passage will be read sentence by sentence, or phrase by phrase, with intervals of 15 seconds. The last reading will be done at normal speed again and during this time you should check your work. You will then be given 2 minutes to check through your work once more.

Read the following passage and choose the correct word from the following table.

A. hearts	I. lunar
B. related	J. sharing
C. linked	K. pandemic
D. gratitude	L. disease
E. jar	M. natural
F. eighth	N. shared
G. traditional	O. safety
H. thick	

  Eight overseas students from Kyrgyzstan, Pakistan and other countries cooked Laba congee—a (1) _____ rice porridge—on Wednesday to express gratitude for the teachers who helped them get through 2020 and the difficulties of the corona virus (2) _____.

  Laba Festival falls on the (3) _____ day of the 12th month on the Chinese (4) _____ calendar. It's (5) _____ to cook congee, a porridge made by boiling rice in water until it acquires a pudding-like consistency. It is (6) _____ with family and friends to welcome the new year.

  "With the coming of Laba, we wish everyone (7) _____ and especially thank our teachers, who helped us a lot in the past year," said Aibek Nurlanbekov, an international student from Kyrgyzstan who studies international trade at Liaoning University.

  In China, food and festivals are often (8) _____, and the food carries good wishes. Aibek and the other international students bought high-quality grains online from Liaoning province. They cooked the Laba congee together to thank their teachers for helping them spend the year 2020 safely and in good health.

  "We are also grateful to share congee with our students. They may not speak

Chinese, but I can feel their (9) _____ . This is not only a pot of congee but also a symbol of (10) _____ and love for China," said Jiang Tao, head of the Institute of International Education at the university.

Summary.

*Listen to the passage and complete the notes using **no more than** three words for each blank.*

The Mid-Autumn Festival is an important festival in some Asian countries. Because the date of this festival is set according to the _____, the precise date varies from year to year. _____ and eating moon cakes are traditional customs of this festival. People often _____ moon cakes to family members, colleagues and friends. Some families go outside to gaze at the glowing of _____. In Vietnam, children and adults also light up _____ to celebrate the festival.

Translation.

Translate the following paragraphs into English or Chinese.

灯笼起源于东汉，最初主要用于照明。在唐代，人们用红灯笼来庆祝安定的生活。从那时起，灯笼在中国的许多地方流行起来。灯笼通常用色彩鲜艳的薄纸制作，形状和尺寸各异。在中国传统文化中，红灯笼象征生活美满和生意兴隆，通常在春节、元宵节和国庆等节日期间悬挂。如今，世界上其他许多地方也能看到红灯笼。

Chinese people return home for family reunions during the Spring Festival holiday by tradition. This has led to massive seasonal travel rushes in recent years as lots of people leave their hometowns to seek work elsewhere, known as the Spring Festival travel rush. It is called the world's largest human migration. Major changes have taken place in the last few decades that have made travel much smoother in the country. Although navigating the Spring

Festival travel rush remains a challenge, the path has become less bumpy（颠簸的）, less stressful and less time-consuming thanks to the rapid development of railway transportation.

Writing.

A wave of efforts to carry forward traditional culture is sweeping China nationwide. Starting from hit cultural TV programmes such as Chinese Idioms Congress, Chinese Poetry Conference and the most successful Readers, the richness and depth of Chinese culture are knocking on the doors of people's hearts.

What is your view on this phenomenon? Write an essay in at least 120 words.

Unit 2

Confucian Thoughts

Learning Objectives

After learning this unit, you will be able to:
- learn to introduce Confucius and his general thoughts in English;
- listen to some materials about Confucian thoughts;
- try to understand more about Confucian thoughts in detail, especially "Ren" and "Li";
- learn and appreciate the English translation of the *Analects of Confucius*.

Confucius (551 BC–479 BC), a scholar and teacher, lived in a chaotic and violent time in China. The name "Confucius" is a Latinized form of the Mandarin Chinese Kung Fuzi ("Master Kong"), and was coined in the late 16th century by the early Jesuit missionaries to China. He wished to see peace and harmony restored and a return to order. Confucius's objective of social and political harmony for China rested on three major foundations: self-cultivation, respect  for rituals and traditions, and the importance of human relationships. His teachings, (the *Analects of Confucius*), collected and recorded by adherents after his death, were foundational for traditional Chinese formal and informal education, and continue to influence contemporary Chinese and East Asian cultures. Traditional Confucianism stressed the importance of five human relationships in particular: parent–child, husband–wife, older sibling–younger sibling, friend–friend, and ruler–subject. Confucius viewed almost all human relationships as hierarchical and reciprocal. Educational attainment was particularly valued. Shihuangdi, the first emperor of China's initial dynasty, the Qin, and his legalist advisers targeted Confucian scholars and books in an effort to crush the opposition. Several hundred years after his death, Confucius's teachings rose to prominence under Emperor Wudi (156 BC–87 BC) during the Han dynasty (206 BC–220 AD). Confucianism laid the groundwork for a central government civil service and, though not the only Chinese belief system, profoundly emphasized Chinese perceptions of ethical and unethical behavior.

 Lead-in

*Watch a short video of **Confucius** and decide whether the statements are true (T) or false (F).*

1. Confucius was the founder of Daoism. _____
2. The *Analects of Confucius* was recorded and compiled by students of Confucius. _____
3. Confucius was the first teacher who taught large numbers of students in a private capacity. _____
4. Confucius advocated that men have equal rights to be educated and should be taught according to their aptitude. _____
5. Confucius is the Latinized name of a person who has been known in China as Kongzi or Kongfuzi. _____

Work in groups and discuss the following questions.

- What does Confucius advocate in teaching?
- How many students did Confucius teach?
- What is the core of Confuciu's opinion?
- What is the representative of the Confucian culture?

Part II Reading

Confucian Thoughts

An Educator, A Giver

Confucius (551 BC−479 BC), or Kong Zi, was a Chinese political figure, philosopher and educator of the Spring and Autumn Period (770 BC−476 BC). He was also the founder of Confucianism (Ru School) and one of the most well-known cultural celebrities throughout the world.

Confucius' surname is Kong, his given name is Qiu, and his social name is Zhongni. He lived in the State of Lu, somewhere near the present Nanxin town of Qufu city in Southeastern Shandong province.

He edited the court chronicle of Lu State, the *Spring and Autumn Annals*, and his teachings, conversations as well as exchanges with his **disciples** are recorded in the *Analects of Confucius*.

disciple [dɪ'saɪpl]
n. 门徒，弟子

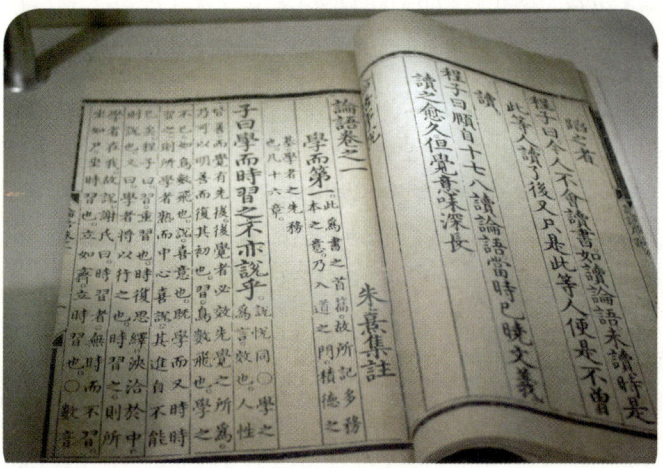

In the time that Confucius lived, education was exclusive to the nobility. Confucius was the first person in ancient Chinese history that offered free education to others.

It is widely believed that Confucius taught over 3,000 disciples in his life, with 72 of them **mastering** his philosophy and **excelling** in the Six Arts.

The Six Arts

The Six Arts, which already existed before Confucianism, are:

- Ritual
- Music
- Archery
- Driving (Carriage)
- Calligraphy
- Mathematics

The *Analects of Confucius*

Confucius' teachings, sayings and life stories are recorded by his disciples and their students in the *Analects of Confucius*, also known as *Lunyu*.

Over 2,000 years later, The *Analects of Confucius* is now being studied and quoted throughout the world across all industries. To this day, the *Analects of Confucius* is still one of the most widely read and studied books in China, and it continues to have a strong influence on Chinese values today.

Confucius' Impact on Modern Philosophy

Confucius believed that all people should have a **sound** character with an **uplifting mindset**. He encouraged his disciples to be givers and contributors to their society and

---

master ['mɑːstə(r)] *v.* 掌握；控制

excel [ɪk'sel] *v.* 擅长，突出；胜过

sound [saʊnd] *adj.* 明智的；透彻的；健康的

uplifting [ˌʌp'lɪftɪŋ] *adj.* 令人振奋的；使人开心的

mindset ['maɪndset] *n.* 观念模式，思维倾向，心态

take on more social responsibility. "Simply knowing the highest standards of virtue is not as good as setting it as one's goal. Setting it as one's goal is not as good as enjoying the practice of it."

Modern scholars believe Confucius to be the pioneer in thinking that increasing one's knowledge is not the ultimate goal, but the process of broadening their perspective and living spiritually is. This builds the foundation of the point of view on life in modern Chinese philosophy.

The Origin of Ren

The character "仁" was first created by combining "亻" and "二".

The left part of "仁" is "亻", which means a man who is standing. In 1200 BC–1050 BC, it was written in the oracle bone script:

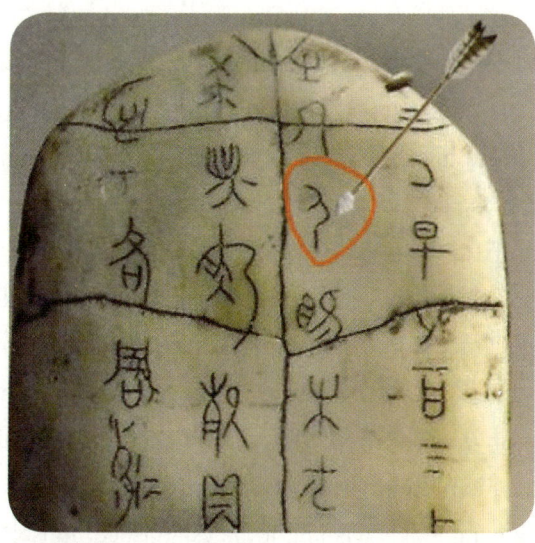

The right part of Ren is "二", representing heaven and the earth.

The Meaning of Ren

In ancient China, Ren, as the moral **realm**, had a wide range of meanings. The concept of Ren was mentioned 109 times in the Analects. The original meaning of Ren is "the closeness between people", from the ancient Chinese dictionary *Shuowen Jiezi*.

Ren and Li are two principal concepts of Confucianism. The core thought of Confucianism is Ren. There have been a variety of definitions for the term Ren. Ren has been translated as "benevolence", "perfect virtue", "goodness", "humaneness" or even "human-heartedness". When asked, Confucius simply explains in the Analects as "Love of people". It also "begins with the love of one's parents". Ren is exemplified by a normal adult's protective feelings for children. It is considered the inward expression of Confucian ideals.

As for love for other people other than your parents, Confucius explained: "Do not do toward others anything you would not want to be done to you." This is now commonly known as the golden rule of Confucius.

Yan Hui, Confucius's most outstanding student, once asked his master to describe the rules of Ren and Confucius replied, "One should see nothing improper, hear nothing improper, say nothing improper, do nothing improper." Confucian value of Ren: "To **subdue** oneself and return to propriety, is perfect virtue." Confucius also defined Ren in the following way: "wishing to be established himself, also seeks to establish others; wishing to be enlarged himself, he also seeks to enlarge others." Another meaning of Ren is "not

---

realm [relm] *n.*
领域，范围

subdue [səbˈdjuː]
vt. 征服；克制；制服

to do to others as you would not wish done to yourself." Confucius also said, "Ren is not far off; he who seeks it has already found it." Ren is close to a man and never leaves him.

In Chinese culture, Ren is considered the most important moral standard by Confucius, thus forming the core of the Chinese ethical system. For example, 仁爱孝悌: Benevolence and filial piety；亲仁善邻,国之宝也: Benevolence and good-neighbourliness are of great value to the country.

Nature of Ren

Ren relies heavily on the relationships between two people, but at the same time, **encompasses** much more than that. It represents an inner development towards an **altruistic** goal, while **simultaneously** realizing that one is never alone, and that everyone has these relationships to **fall back on**, being a member of a family, the state, and the world.

Confucianism places a large importance on relationships. There are the Five Bonds:
- ruler to ruled
- father and son
- husband and wife
- elder brother to younger brother
- friend to friend

Confucianism also places a heavy emphasis on the optimistic view of human nature. Confucianism truly believes in humanity and that humans can become amazing. Confucius believes that humans are "teachable, improvable,

encompass [ɪn'kʌmpəs] vt. 围绕，包围；包含或包括某事物；完成
altruistic [ˌæltru'ɪstɪk] adj. 利他的，无私心的
simultaneously [ˌsɪməl'teɪniəsli] adv. 同时地；一齐
fall back on 求助于，依赖，转而依靠

and perfectible" through proper ethical and philosophical training.

Ren is not a concept that is learned; it is **innate**; that is to say, everyone is born with the sense of Ren. Confucius believed that the key to long-lasting **integrity** was to constantly think, since the world is continually changing at a rapid pace.

Ren also has a political dimension. Confucianism says that if the ruler lacks Ren, it will be difficult for his **subjects** to behave humanely. Ren is the basis of Confucian political theory; the ruler is **exhorted** to **refrain** from acting inhumanely towards his subjects. An inhumane ruler runs the risk of losing the **Mandate** of Heaven or, in other words, the right to rule. A ruler lacking such a mandate need not be obeyed, but a ruler who **reigns** humanely and takes care of the people is to be obeyed, for the benevolence of his dominion shows that he has been mandated by heaven. Confucius himself had little to say on the active will of the people, though he believed the ruler should definitely pay attention to the wants and needs of the people and take good care of them. Mencius, however, did state that the people's opinions on certain weighty matters should be polled.

Modern scholars believe ren represents an **all-encompassing** sense of virtue, which is the basis for growing into **ethically** well-cultivated men.

Li and the Five Basic Virtues of Confucianism

Li, the Confucian concepts are often **rendered** as "ritual", "proper conduct", or "propriety". The *Analects of Confucius* records how Confucius explains this: The purpose of Li is to maintain harmonious human relationships. It further explains the details of Li, which includes proper manners, **rituals**, customs and traditions that are considered norms or standards of an ideal Confucian society.

Confucius explains that it is not through the **suppression** of individual desires that we achieve a harmonious society, but rituals and norms should be established and taught to **reconcile** people's desires. Only so, will people carry themselves with **dignity** and **demonstrate** the highest degree of integrity in all things.

Including Li, the following are the Five Virtues of Confucianism:

- Ren: love and respect of people, benevolence
- Li: proper manners, rituals, customs and traditions
- Yi: justice and righteousness
- Zhi: knowledge and wisdom
- Xin: integrity and fidelity

Principles of Ren, Li, and Yi

The principle of Ren is related to the concepts of Li and Yi. Li is often translated as "ritual" while Yi is often translated as "righteousness". These three interrelated terms deal with the **agency** as Confucians **conceive** it. Li is the action that has been **deemed** appropriate by society, Yi is the action that is indeed correct, while ren deals with the relationship between the agent and object of the action. Often Li and Yi are the same; however, that is not always the case.

Li is the outward expression of Confucian ideals, while Ren is both the inward and outward expressions of those same ideals. According to Hopfe and Woodward (Authors of the *Religions of the World*): "Basically, Li seems to mean 'the course of life as it is intended to go.' Li also has religious and social connotations. When a society lives by Li, it moves smoothly: men and women respect their elders and superiors; the proper rituals and ceremonies are performed; everything and everyone is in its proper place."

Famous Quotes by Confucius

Learning without thought is labor lost; thought without learning is perilous.（学而不思则罔，思而不学则殆。）

When I walk with two men, they may serve me as my teachers. I will select their good qualities and follow them, while select their bad qualities and avoid them.（三人行，必有我师焉。择其善者而从之，其不善者而改之。）

When you know a thing, to hold that you know it; and when you do not know a thing, to allow that you do not know it—this is knowledge.（知之为知之，不知为不知，是知也。）

Reading Comprehension.

Choose the best answer according to the text.

1. The *Analects of Confucius* were written by _____.

    A. Confucius himself

    B. Confucius and his disciples or students

    C. Confucius's disciples and their followers

    D. Mencius

2. The central theme of Confucius's thought is _____.

    A. ritual   B. love

C. wisdom   D. faithfulness

3. Which is the following ways of translation incorrect?

   A. 礼之用，和为贵。The role of proprieties is to maintain harmony among people.

   B. 己所不欲，勿施于人。Do toward others anything you would not want to be done to you.

   C. 泛爱众。Universal love.

   D. 仁者，人也，亲亲为大。The greatest love for people is the love for parents.

4. According to Confucius, human love starts from _____.

   A. a universal love

   B. a harmonious society

   C. a peaceful life

   D. intimate feelings between parents and their children

5. All of the following are the ways of translation of the famous saying "克己复礼" EXCEPT _____.

   A. to discipline the self and observe the ritual propriety

   B. to restrain one's desire and restore the traditions of the Zhou dynasty

   C. to do whatever one wants to do

   D. to subdue oneself and return to propriety

6. Confucius' principal interest was in _____.

   A. the meaning of nature

   B. the meaning of Dao

   C. the relationship between nature and human beings

   D. the relationships among individuals

7. For Confucius, the relationship between father and son is fundamental because _____.

   A. women were not as important as men in Confucius's times

   B. the relationship cultivated one's behavior into family reverence which led to universal love and a harmonious society

C. few people understood the relationship and family members fought against each other for money

D. none of the above

Part III Listening and Speaking

Confucian Teaching

Three Confucian Values

Robert Oxnam: Confucian teaching rests on three essential values: Filial piety, humaneness, and ritual.

Irene Bloom: The Confucian value system may be likened in some ways to a tripod, which is one of the great vessels of the Shang and Zhou Periods and a motif that reoccurs in later Chinese art. You could say of the three legs of the tripod. One is filial devotion, or filial piety. A second is humaneness. A third is ritual or ritual consciousness.

Filial Piety (Xiao)

Robert Oxnam: Respect for one's parents, filial piety, is considered the most fundamental of the Confucian values, the root of all others.

Wm. Theodore de Bary: Almost everyone is familiar with the idea that filial piety is a prime virtue in Confucianism. It's a prime virtue in the sense that, from the Confucian point of view, it's the starting point of virtue. Humaneness is the ultimate goal, is the larger vision, but it starts with filial piety.

> Few of those who are filial sons and respectful brothers will show disrespect to superiors, and there has never been a man who is

respectful to superiors and yet creates disorder. A superior man is devoted to the fundamental. When the root is firmly established, the moral law will grow. Filial piety and brotherly respect are the root of humanity.

[*Excerpt from the Analects of Confucius*]

Robert Oxnam: Filial piety derives from that most fundamental human bond: parent and child. The parent-child relationship is appropriately the first of the five Confucian relationships. Although the child is the junior member in the relationship, the notion of reciprocity is still key to understanding filial piety. The Chinese word for this is Xiao.

Irene Bloom: The top portion of the Chinese character for Xiao shows an old man and underneath, a young man supporting the old man. There is this sense of the support by the young of the older generation and the respect of the young for the older generation, but it's also reciprocal. Just as parents have looked after children in their infancy and nurtured them, so the young are supposed to look after parents when they have reached old age and to revere them and to sacrifice to them after their death as well.

Humaneness (Ren)

Robert Oxnam: Another key value in Confucian thinking—the second leg of the tripod—is humaneness, the care and concern for other human beings.

Irene Bloom: A second, very important concept in the *Analects of Confucius*, and again in later Confucian thought, is that of Ren. Sometimes that term Ren is translated as goodness, benevolence. I prefer to translate it as humaneness or humanity because the Chinese character is made up of two parts.

On the left is the element that means a person or a human being. On the right the element that represents the number two. So, Ren has a sense of a person together with others. A human being together with other human beings, a human being in society.

> *Confucius said: "...The humane man, desiring to be established himself, seeks to establish others; desiring himself to succeed, he helps others to succeed. To judge others by what one knows of oneself is the method of achieving humanity..."*
>
> [*Excerpt from the Analects of Confucius*]

Ritual (Li)

Robert Oxnam: The last of the three central Confucian values is "respect for ritual"—the proper way of doing things in the deepest sense.

Irene Bloom: The third leg in this tripod is that of Li—ritual consciousness or **propriety**. Li represents the forms in which human actions are supposed to go on.

> *Confucius said*: "*In rites at large, it is always better to be too simple rather than too lavish. In funeral rites, it is more important to have the real sentiment of sorrow than minute attention to observances.*"
>
> [*Excerpt from the Analects of Confucius*]

Irene Bloom: In the Chinese character Li, the strong religious associations are very, very clear here. On the left side of the character Li is the element indicating prognostication or presaging. On the right, you have a ritual vessel.

So while in the course of evolution of the Confucian tradition, Li, rights, are considered to have become more, what in the West might be called more secular in character, not to be concerned so much with the idea of trying to appease deceased ancestors as had been true in the period prior to the time of Confucius. Still the notion of the ritual retains a very strong religious association throughout time.

Wm. Theodore de Bary: So as that evolves in a more secular, humanistic context, it still retains the sense that individuals have to defer to one another, have to show respect to one another. They have to be prepared to make some sacrifice for one another.

Myron Cohen: Confucius himself emphasized again and again that ritual itself was important. That rituals, that through ritual, people could learn proper relationships.

So if we look at ancestor worship through the lenses of ritual, what can we see? We can see, first of all, that through ancestor worship filial piety is eternal. People can continue to be loyal and obedient to their parents even after their parents have passed away.

At the same time, and in line, indeed, with the ancient Confucian theory, through ancestor worship, parents continue to teach their own children filial piety.

On Education

Robert Oxnam: Implicit in the Confucian emphasis on ritual and self-cultivation through ritual is the notion that life is a continuous process of learning and self-improvement. Confucius stressed the importance of education for achieving personal and social order.

When Confucius was traveling to Wei, Ran Yu drove him.

Confucius observed, "What a dense population!"

Ran Yu said, "The people having grown so numerous, what next should be done for them?"

"Enrich them," was the reply.

"And when one has enriched them, what next should be done?"

Confucius said, "Educate them."

[*Excerpt from the Analects of Confucius*]

What Were the Confucian Classics?

The oldest listing of the Five Classics dates from 200 BC.

★ *Book of History* (*Shu Jing*)—The historical records of the early Chinese dynasties.

★ *Book of Songs* (*Shi Jing*)—A 600 BC collection of lyric poems composed between ca. 1000 BC−600 BC.

★ *Book of Rites* (*Li Jing*)— A guide to proper ritual behavior.

★ *Book of Changes* (*Yi Jing*)—A book of diagrams with interpretations passed on since the early Zhou dynasty for use in prognostication.

★ *Spring and Autumn Annals* (*Chun Qiu*)—The annals of the state of Lu, said to be recorded each spring and autumn, reporting significant events during the period 770 BC−476 BC (hence the name for this era, "Spring and Autumn Period").

The Four Books were added to the list of classics during the Han dynasty.

★ *Analects of Confucius* (*Lun Yu*)—The sayings and conversations of Confucius, collected by his followers.

★ *Great Learning* (*Da Xue*)—The concept of virtuous government with commentaries.

★ *Doctrine of the Mean* (*Zhong Yong*)—A guide, ascribed to Confucius' grandson, for achieving mental balance and harmony in one's life according to the Confucian principle of seeking regulation and moderation in all things.

★ *Mencius* (*Mengzi*)—The conversations of Confucius' most famous follower, Mencius, were collected by his own followers.

Is Confucian Thought "Religious"?

Robert Oxnam: The question is often raised as to whether or not Confucian thought should be considered "religious".

Irene Bloom: As Confucianism is understood in the West, it often seems to come with a little tag attached saying, "This is

philosophical and not religious." Which raises some very interesting questions about the nature of religion. What constitutes religion?

Wm. Theodore de Bary: According to Western conceptions of religion, primarily based upon the prophetic traditions of the Old and New Testament, or the Koran, certainly Confucianism is not a religion.

But nevertheless, Confucius has a very, very strong sense of reverence towards heaven, which is not distinguishable from a reverence towards life. You have a reverence towards life, and heaven is the source of life.

Irene Bloom: Confucius also draws on the authority of Heaven. The Chinese word, Tian, can actually be translated either as heaven or as nature. But it has a sense of a moral order existing in the world, which governs all of human life and all of the processes of the natural world at the same time. Confucius says at one point, "Heaven gave birth to the power that is in me"—the power or the virtue that is in me. He seems to regard heaven as overseeing his life and the lives of others and overseeing, also, the cause of culture, so that there's a certain confidence here.

> *Confucius said: "I wish I did not have to speak at all."*
>
> *Zi Gong said: "But if you did not speak, Sir, what should we disciples pass on to others?"*
>
> *Confucius said: "Look at Heaven there. Does it speak? The four seasons run their course and all things are produced. Does Heaven speak?"*
>
> [*Excerpt from the Analects of Confucius*]

Irene Bloom: Heaven does not speak, human beings have to discover the ways, the patterns, the order of heaven as it works out in the larger world of society and in their own lives.

Wm. Theodore de Bary: So what I would say is that Confucius and Confucianism have a very strong religious dimension, but they pretty much assume that the basics of religion are already given in the pre-existing tradition.

Robert Oxnam: This pre-existing tradition assumed that there is a cosmic order and that it is moral. Furthermore, this moral order was assumed to extend through the cosmos at every level—in heaven, on earth, and in human society.

Myron Cohen: The point is that these were not distinguished as separate domains, but as interconnected domains. It's this holistic interconnected, cosmic, integrated, entire view that I think is a fundamental characteristic of Chinese thought and Chinese belief in general, such that Confucianism fits into it.

For example, the basic Confucian ideas of filial piety—that children must be loyal and obedient to their parents, show them respect in life and reverence after they have died—these are not simply ethical ideas. These were ethical ideas given, if you will, cosmic validation. That a son should be respectful of his father was seen to be as much a part of nature as the rising and setting of the sun. So that ethical relationships were thought to be natural relationships.

Therefore, violating an ethical relationship would seem to be violating nature itself. The sanctions were natural, not supernatural, because in effect, you were causing disorder in the cosmos by violating ethical relationships. And this notion of the cosmos as containing important human relationships, as well as relationships and phenomena which we in the West might consider to be part of nature and distinct from human relationships, extended to many, many areas of thinking in China.

About the Speakers

1. *William Theodore de Bary*

John Mitchell Mason Professor Emeritus; Provost Emeritus; Special Service Professor Columbia University

2. *Irene Bloom*

Anne Whitney Olin Professor Emerita Columbia University

3. *Myron L. Cohen*

Professor, Department of Anthropology; Director, Weatherhead East Asian Institute Columbia University

4. *Robert B. Oxnam*

President Emeritus Asia Society

New Words

likened	[ˈlaɪkənd]	v. 把……比作
tripod	[ˈtraɪpɒd]	n. 三足鼎
vessel	[ˈvesl]	n. 容器
motif	[məʊˈtiːf]	n.（文艺作品等的）主题
reciprocity	[ˌresɪˈprɒsəti]	n. 相互性；相互作用
reciprocal	[rɪˈsɪprəkl]	adj. 相互的；互惠的
nurture	[ˈnɜːtʃə(r)]	vt. 养育；培育
revere	[rɪˈvɪə(r)]	vt. 崇敬；尊崇
sacrifice	[ˈsækrɪfaɪs]	v. 牺牲；舍弃
lavish	[ˈlævɪʃ]	adj. 过分丰富的
prognostication	[prɒgˌnɒstɪˈkeɪʃn]	n. 预言
presaging	[ˈpresɪdʒɪŋ]	n. 预示，预兆

续表

New Words		
secular	[ˈsekjələ(r)]	adj. 现世的，俗界的
appease	[əˈpiːz]	v. 平息；安抚，抚慰
lenses	[lensɪz]	n. 透镜，镜头（lens的名词复数）
implicit	[ɪmˈplɪsɪt]	adj. 不言明［含蓄］的；无疑问的，绝对的
annal	[ˈænl]	n. 记录
cosmos	[ˈkɒzmɒs]	n. 宇宙
reverence	[ˈrevərəns]	n. 尊敬，敬畏
distinguishable	[dɪˈstɪŋgwɪʃəbl]	adj. 可以区别开的，可辨别的
New Phrases		
derive from		由……起源；取自
at large		一般说来；详细地
defer to		遵从；听从
Proper Name		
Koran	[kəˈrɑːn]	n.《古兰经》（伊斯兰教）

Listening Comprehension.

Decide whether the statements are true (T) or false (F) according to the passage.

1. Humaneness is considered the most fundamental of Confucian values. _____

2. Respect for one's parents, is the starting point of virtue and the ultimate goal. _____

3. The parent-child relationship is the first of the five Confucian relationships. _____

4. Ren is a very important concept in the *Analects of Confucius*, and can be translated as goodness, benevolence, etc. _____
5. Confucius thought simplicity is better than trivial formalities in rites. _____
6. According to Confucius's Li, children should be obedient to their parents even after their parents have passed away. _____
7. Confucius stressed the importance of education for achieving personal and social order. _____
8. In order to achieve social order, Confucius emphasized education and self-cultivation. _____
9. The classics have an important influence on ancient China, but it doesn't work for modern Chinese people. _____
10. Confucianism is philosophical and religious. It has a strong sense for Chinese people. _____

Work in groups to discuss the following questions.

- What are the three essential values in Confucian teaching?
- Why did Irene Bloom translate Ren as humaneness?
- How do you understand Xiao, Ren, Li?
- What were the Confucian classics?
- Is Confucian thought "religious"?
- How do you understand Tian?

Part IV Further Reading

Confucius's Philosophy Quoted by Foreign Dignitaries

President Xi Jinping became the first Chinese president to address an international meeting about the ancient Chinese philosopher Confucius (551 BC–479 BC) on Wednesday.

Confucianism, a system developed from Confucius' thoughts, is an ethical and philosophical system, which has become an influential part of Chinese culture.

A rich literary heritage of Confucianism has been left to the Chinese known as the Four Books and Five Classics: *Great Learning*, *Doctrine of the Mean*, *Analects of Confucius*, and *Mencius*; *Book of Change*, *Book of History*, *Book of Songs*, *Book of Rites* and *Spring and Autumn Annals*.

Confucianism means a lot not only to China, but also to the world. In 1988, 75 Nobel prizewinners said that if mankind is to survive, it must go back 25 centuries in time to tap the wisdom of Confucius.

Today, extracts from Confucianism are frequently quoted by foreign dignitaries in their speeches or talks.

UN Secretary-General Ban Ki-moon mentioned in 2014 at Nanjing University that one of the very important guidelines for him was the Confucian tradition. When talking about his decision to dedicate himself to public service, he cited a teaching of Confucianism in his speech, "Cultivate oneself, put a family in order, govern the state, and pacify the world." (修身齐家治国平天下) Ban Ki-moon explained that, "To put the world in order, you must first put your country in order; but to put the country in order, you must have a very harmonious family; and to put our family harmoniously in order, we must cultivate our personal life."

During US President Barack Obama's town hall meeting in Shanghai in

2009, he cited the saying coined by Confucius, "Consider the past and you shall know the future"(温故而知新), to express that the two countries should learn from the past to develop Sino-US diplomatic relations in the new era.

Former Russian president Dmitry Medvedev made a speech at Peking University in 2008, spicing it with references to Chinese philosophers Confucius and Laozi. When speaking of education, he cited Confucius' "Learn and practice often what you have learned, isn't it pleasant?"(学而时习之，不亦说乎) to express his favor of Chinese education methods.

Former president of Germany Johannes Rau visited Nanjing University in 2003. In a ceremony in which he received an honorary doctorate from the university, he quoted what Confucius told his disciple about politics, "If a government is not trustworthy, its people cannot rely on it."(民无信不立)

During former French president Valery Giscard d'Estaing's visit to Qufu, Shandong province in 2004, he recited a few pieces of famous instruction from Confucius in Chinese, such as "devoted and love antiquity"(信而好古) to express his respect for the wise men in the past.

The whole sentence by Confucius is "To relate and not to invent, devoted and love antiquity, I strive to be like Laozi (a famous Chinese philosopher) and Peng Zhu (an official during the Shang dynasty), to pass down the essence of ancient works."

The Temple of Confucius in Qufu, first built in 478 BC, is the prototype of some 2,000 Confucian temples all over the world, including Japan, the Republic of Korea, the United States, Singapore and Vietnam.

New Words		
address	[ə'dres]	v. 解决；演讲；向……说话；称呼
ethical	['eθɪkl]	adj. 伦理学的；道德的，伦理的

续表

New Words		
coin	[kɔɪn]	v. 创造
diplomatic	[ˌdɪpləˈmætɪk]	adj. 外交（官）的
spice	[spaɪs]	vt. 加香料于；使增添趣味
doctorate	[ˈdɒktərət]	n. 博士学位
antiquity	[ænˈtɪkwəti]	n. 古代；古物；古代的风俗习惯
prototype	[ˈprəʊtətaɪp]	n. 原型，雏形，蓝本
Proper Names		
Ban Ki-moon		潘基文（联合国前秘书长）
Barack Obamat		贝拉克·奥巴马（美国前总统）
Dmitry Medvedev		德米特里·梅德韦杰夫（俄罗斯前总统）
Johannes Rau		约翰内斯·劳（德国前总统）
Valery Giscard d'Estaing		瓦莱里·吉斯卡尔·德斯坦（法国前总统）

Reading Comprehension.

Fill in the blanks according to the news.

Confucianism, a system developed from Confucius' (1) _____, is an ethical and philosophical system, which has become an (2) _____ part of Chinese culture. In the Four Books and Five Classics was recorded the (3) _____ of Confucianism. Confucianism means a lot not only to China, but also to the world. The (4) _____ of Confucius can be traced back to 25 centuries ago. A teaching of Confucianism "Cultivate oneself, put a family in order, govern the state, and pacify the world" means we must (5) _____ our personal life in order to build a (6) _____ family, country and world. "Consider the past and you shall know the future" used in the two countries means that we should learn from the past to develop Sino-US

(7) _____ relations in the new era. When speaking of education, Confucius said "Learn and practice often what you have learned, isn't it (8) _____ ?" About politics, Confucius told his disciple: "If a government is not (9) _____ , its people cannot rely on it." To express his respect for the wise men in the past, Confucius said "devoted and love antiquity" to pass down the (10) _____ of ancient works.

 Viewing

*Watch a short video of **Filial Piety** and discuss the following questions.*

- What is filial piety?
- How to show filial piety to our parents?

Part VI Appreciation

Please appreciate the following translation from the Analects of Confucius.

1. 学而时习之，不亦说乎？有朋自远方来，不亦乐乎？人不知而不愠，不亦君子乎？

   To learn and then repeat and practice what you have learned at due times—is this not a pleasure? To have men of kindred spirit come from afar—is this not delightful? Is he not a man of virtue who harbours no resentment though others do not appreciate him?

2. 君子务本，本立而道生。孝弟也者，其为仁之本与！

   The man of virtue devotes himself to what is radical, and when it has been established the Way evolves. Filial devotion and respect for elders are, perhaps, the root of all virtuous conducts.

3. 巧言令色，鲜矣仁。

   Clever words and an ingratiating manner are seldom emissions of virtuous character.

4. 唯仁者能好人，能恶人。

   It is the benevolent man alone who is capable of liking or disliking other men.

5. 弟子入则孝，出则悌，谨而信，泛爱众而亲仁。

   A young man should be a good son at home and an obedient young man abroad, sparing of speech but trustworthy in what he says, and should love the multitude at large but cultivate the friendship of his fellow men.

6. 能以礼让为国乎，何有？

   For a man who is able to govern a state by observing the rites and showing deference, what is there to hold office?

7. 知者乐水，仁者乐山。知者动，仁者静。知者乐，仁者寿。

   The wise find joy in water; the benevolent find joy in mountains. The wise are active; the benevolent are still. The wise are joyful; the benevolent are long-lived.

8. 事父母，几谏，见志不从，又敬不违，劳而不怨。

   In serving your father and mother you ought to dissuade them from doing wrong in the gentlest way. If you see your advice being ignored, you should not become disobedient but should remain reverent. You should not complain even if you are distressed.

9. 刚、毅、木、讷，近仁。

   Unbending strength, resoluteness, simplicity and slowness of speech are close to benevolence.

10. 今之孝者，是谓能养。至于犬马，皆能有养，不敬，何以别乎？

    Nowadays, to provide parents with enough food is considered being filial. But dogs and horses are also provided to that extent. Without reverence, what is the difference?

11. 子曰："父母在，不远行，游必有方。"

    The Master said, "While your parents are alive, you should not travel too far afield. If you do travel, your whereabouts should always be known."

12. 父母之年，不可不知也。一则以喜，一则以惧。

    Children should think often of the age of their parents. They should feel happy. They should also feel concerned.

13. 孝悌也者，其为仁之本与！

    To have love for parents and respect for elder brothers is the trunk or essence of filial piety.

14. 仁者，人也，亲亲为大。

    The greatest love for people is the love for parents.

15. 己所不欲，勿施于人。

Do not do toward others anything you would not want to be done to you.

 Practising

Decide whether the statements are true (T) or false (F).

1. The *Analects of Confucius*, a book about Confucius's words and deeds, was written by Confucius himself. _____
2. Many of Confucius's teachings are concerned with human affairs. _____
3. Humaneness comes from family reverence which is cultivated through the intimate relationship between parents and their children. _____
4. According to Confucius, humane love for others is of the first importance while propriety comes secondary. _____
5. Behavior cultivation from family reverence to the social relationship is the only way to fulfill a man. _____
6. To have love for parents and respect for elder brothers is the central theme of ren. _____
7. The most important governing principle is to apply laws to people. _____
8. Li or propriety can be followed without Ren (love or humaneness). _____
9. In the usage of ritual, "it is harmony that is prized" means rites are observed to achieve harmony. _____
10. It seems that li is the standard and norm for the judgment of one's mental and physical actions. _____

Choose the correct translation from the following choices.

1. 孝悌也者，其为仁之本与！

    A. The greatest love for people is the love for parents.

    B. Do not do toward others anything you would not want to be done to you.

C. To have love for parents and respect for elder brothers is the trunk or essence of filial piety.

2. 仁者，人也，亲亲为大。

   A. The greatest love for people is the love for parents.

   B. Do not do toward others anything you would not want to be done to you.

   C. To have love for parents and respect for elder brothers is the trunk or essence of filial piety.

3. 己所不欲，勿施于人。

   A. The greatest love for people is the love for parents.

   B. Do not do toward others anything you would not want to be done to you.

   C. To have love for parents and respect for elder brothers is the trunk or essence of filial piety.

Match the teachings of Confucius in Section A with the English translations in Section B.

Section A

1. 唯仁者能好人，能恶人。 _____
2. 弟子入则孝，出则悌，谨而信，泛爱众而亲仁。 _____
3. 仁者，人也，亲亲为大。 _____
4. 知者乐水，仁者乐山。知者动，仁者静。知者乐，仁者寿。 _____
5. 己所不欲，勿施于人。 _____
6. 刚、毅、木、讷，近仁。 _____

Section B

A. The greatest love for people is the love for parents.

B. It is the benevolent man alone who is capable of liking or disliking other men.

C. A young man should be a good son at home and an obedient young man abroad, sparing of speech but trustworthy in what he says, and should love the multitude at large but cultivate the friendship of his fellow men.

D. Do not do toward others anything you would not want to be done to you.

E. Unbending strength, resoluteness, simplicity and slowness of speech are close to benevolence.

F. The wise find joy in water; the benevolent find joy in mountains. The wise are active; the benevolent are still. The wise are joyful; the benevolent are long-lived.

Translation.

Translate the following paragraphs into English or Chinese.

《论语》是儒家学派的经典著作（classics）之一。该书记录了（records）孔子及其弟子的言行，传授儒家的主要思想（central theme）：仁、义（righteousness）、礼、智，其中仁是儒家的核心价值观（kernel value）。仁是指爱父母和敬长兄，如果这种对家庭成员的情感延伸（extend to）到社会的其他人身上，人与人之间和睦关系也就建立起来了。

Confucianism is an early collection of ethics and social and philosophical ideas that are based upon the teachings of the ancient Chinese philosopher Confucius. The basic idea of Confucianism is how each person can participate in creating a peaceful, well-organized society. Confucianism stresses the importance of individual relationships, basically, how people relate to each other in terms of their place in society. Confucianism actually discourages seeking profit—Confucius said that it led people to do wrong to other people. That idea wouldn't be a good thing to apply to a business.

Writing.

Please choose one of the following topics and write a composition of at least 100 words.

    1. About Confucius.

    2. What could you learn from the *Analects of Confucius*?

Unit 3

Laozi's Philosophy

Learning Objectives

After learning this unit, you will be able to:
- learn to introduce Laozi and his general thoughts in English;
- read some materials about Laozi and understand the philosophy of non-action;
- try to remember the keywords and expressions.

Laozi was an ancient Chinese philosopher. According to Chinese tradition, Laozi lived in the 600 BC, however many historians contend that Laozi actually lived in the 400 BC, which was the period of Hundred Schools of Thought and Warring States Period, while others contend he was a mythical figure. Laozi was credited with writing that seminal Taoist (or Daoist) work, the *Tao Te Ching*, which was originally known as the *Laozi, Daodejing*. Taishang Laojun was a title for Laozi in the Taoist religion.

Part 1 Lead-in

*Watch a short video of **Laozi** and discuss the following questions.*

- Who's the teacher of Confucius?
- What does Laozi believe?
- How do you understand the sentence "water gives life to others, but does not fight with others"? Think about Laozi's philosophy of water.
- Why is Laozi considered the elite of teachers in China?

Reading

Finding Our Way With Laozi

The **legendary** Chinese philosopher Laozi is associated with the long tradition of **Daoism** (or Taoism). But his work is famously **elliptical** and difficult.

Introduction

The *Daodejing* is one of the most translated of all Chinese texts. It is traditionally attributed to the Daoist sage Laozi (also written as Lao Tzu).

At just over 5,000 characters long, the *Daodejing* is a masterpiece of compression. But due to its brevity and its elliptical style, it has been read in a **multitude** of different ways: as everything from a mystical treatise to a hard-headed work about statecraft.

Life

But what about Laozi, the *Daodejing*'s purported author? The name "Laozi" literally means "Old Master". The Chinese tradition says that Laozi's given name was Li Er, and some accounts make him a contemporary of Confucius. However, over the last century scholars have increasingly cast doubt on the historicity of Li Er. And even if there was a historical individual called Li Er, his connection with the *Daodejing* is probably **tenuous**.

The Sage and the Ox

But as usual, where history remains silent, stories **proliferate**. The legendary accounts make Laozi a librarian in the court of Zhou. It was a role that gave him time to read the thoughts of the ancients, and thus cultivate wisdom. The historian Sima Qian tells us Laozi eventually got sick of court life, and at the age of eighty headed west to the frontier regions to live as a **hermit**. At the frontier, a guard apprehended the philosopher, refusing to let him travel onward until he had passed on his wisdom. So Laozi recited the *Daodejing* and the border guard wrote it down. Then the Old Master continued on his way west, riding on the back of an ox, and he was lost to history.

Some accounts even go so far as to say that after heading west from China, Laozi ended up in India, where he became a teacher of the **Buddha**. Like everything else about Laozi's "biography", there is no evidence that any of this is true.

Philosophy: Dao and De

Laozi's text, the *Daodejing*, explores two concepts in particular: dao and de (sometimes written tao and te). Both are tricky to translate, and both are subject to considerable debate. The *Daodejing* begins with the famous sentence:

★ The *dao* that you can *dao* is not the constant *dao*.

The word *dao* in Chinese can mean "way" or "path". But it can also mean "to speak" or "to talk about". So one common way of translating the opening sentence is to take the first and third *dao* as meaning "way" and the second as meaning "to talk about":

★ The way you can talk about is not the constant way.

In this reading, the dao, the natural way of things, is something that escapes all our attempts to speak of it.

But there's a problem here. When translating dao into English as "the" dao, we risk imagining that the dao is some kind of **metaphysical** entity: something big, important and deeply mysterious. However, the definite article does not exist in the original Chinese. So dao can mean the dao, or a dao, or even daos, in the plural. This means that you could also translate the first line as follows:

★ Ways you can talk about are not constant ways.

But there's another level of **ambiguity** as well, because it is possible to read the second *dao* not as "to say" or "to talk about", but as a verb related to the noun "way" or "path". Reading it like this, "to *dao*" would mean something like "to tread a path", "to make your way", or "to lead". This would give us something like the following:

★ Ways you can tread are not constant ways.

If you read it like this, the text might be saying that the paths we take as we make our way through the world—the paths that remain open to us—are always subject to change. You can take a particular path today, but that same path may not be open tomorrow (this recalls Heraclitus's

metaphysical
[ˌmetə'fɪzɪkl] *adj.*
形而上学的；玄学的

ambiguity
[ˌæmbɪ'gjuːəti] *n.*
模棱两可；歧义

claim that you can't step into the same river twice). To keep on moving, if you are a skillful wayfarer, you need to be able to recognize the inconstancy of the paths you are on. You need to be **vigilant**. And you need to be flexible. Because if you rely on a pre-ordained and inflexible *Way*, you will almost certainly stumble.

vigilant
['vɪdʒɪlənt] *adj.*
警觉的

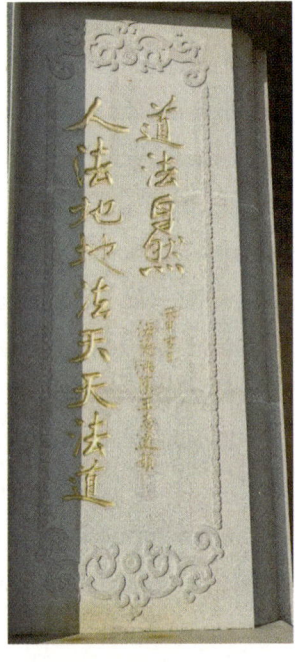

Powers and Potentials

The second concept in the *Daodejing* is de. In texts from the Confucian tradition, de is often translated as "virtue"; but when it comes to Daoist texts like the *Daodejing*, something like "potency" is closer to the mark. So you could read de as the potency or potential that a thing has by virtue of being the kind of thing that it is. The de of a fish is the potential it has to be a fish, to do fishy things. The de of a tree is the potential it has to exist—or even to flourish—as a tree. And so on.

The word de goes back to the Zhou dynasty where,

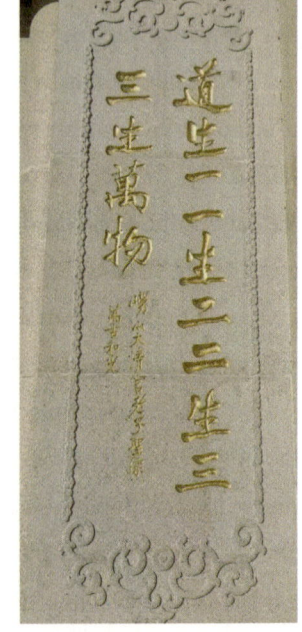

according to the scholar Constance A. Cook, it referred to "a fluid inner force available only to those who participated in the ancestral worship system". By the time the *Daodejing* was written, de had lost its connection with ancestor worship. But it maintained this sense of inner force and **potency**. So if we understand it like this, the aim of the Daodejing is to tell us how to tread paths through an inconstant world while protecting our potency and our force.

potency
['pəʊtnsi] *n.* 影响力；支配力

Unlike virtue, de is not something you practice. The moment you start thinking of de as something to be practiced or something that you do, you lose sight of it. Instead, it is something that comes through allowing your potential to express itself through wuwei or non-action.

For the *Daodejing*, the **optimal** way of being is allowing our *de* to fully express itself by refusing all kinds of forcing and striving. Only when we remove ourselves from striving can our *de*, or potency, be fulfilled. And then, full of life, we can continue in our own idiosyncratic way, making new pathways as we navigate our passage through the world.

optimal
['ɒptɪməl] *adj.* 最优的；最佳的

Reading Comprehension.

Choose the correct answer according to the text.

1. What does the name "Laozi" literally mean?

    A. Old man.　　B. Lao Dan.　　C. Old Master.　　D. Li Er.

2. Why did a guard refuse to let Laozi travel onward at the frontier?

    A. Laozi eventually got sick of court life.

    B. Laozi was a librarian in the court of Zhou.

    C. Laozi had to pass on his wisdom.

    D. Laozi became a teacher of the Buddha.

3. What does the second "Dao" mean in *"The dao that you can dao is not the constant dao"*?

   A. Way.　　　　B. Path.　　　　C. To talk about.　　　　D. Road.

4. What is the *de* of a tree?

   A. The potential it has to exist—or even to flourish—as a tree.

   B. To do fishy things.

   C. Virtue of being the kind of thing that it is.

   D. A fluid inner force.

5. The incorrect description of "de" is _____.

   A. by the time the *Daodejing* was written, de had lost its connection with ancestor worship

   B. like virtue, de is something you practice

   C. the moment you start thinking of de as something to be practiced, you lose sight of it

   D. something that comes through allowing your potential to express itself through wuwei or non-action

Zhuangzi

　　Zhuangzi (369 BC–286 BC), with his given name as Zhou, was a key figure of Taoism following Laozi. He was born at the town of Meng (Northeast of the present-day Shangqiu, Henan province) of the Song State. He once worked as an official in a varnish-free farm before resigning to lead a reclusive life.

　　The book bearing his name has 33 chapters survived. The traditional view is that Zhuangzi penned the first seven "inner" chapters and his disciples and other thinkers contributed the other parts (the "outer" and "miscellaneous" chapters).

　　Similar to Laozi's philosophy, Zhuangzi believed that the "Tao" is the origin of everything in the universe. However, the "Tao" Zhuangzi referred to is an omnipresent and infinite concept in nature.

Zhuangzi transformed Laozi's outlook on life into a spiritual realm of absolute freedom, a "free and easy wandering" state. This state can be achieved, according to Zhuangzi, through a variety of complicated introspective experiences rather than pursuing endless desires in society.

The experience of "xinzhai (mind fasting)" means the freedom from all preoccupations, that is, an attitude free from materialism and a complete unity with nature. By comparing the sophisticated and competitive social reality with the harmonious and tranquil nature, Zhuangzi put forward the notion of "wuhua" (the transformation of things) and appealed to the return of one's suppressed soul back to nature.

Zhuangzi's philosophy of worshipping the nature often leads to the pursuit of a personality of aloofness. The philosophical basis of this aloofness is relativism, that is, in his own words, "The universe and I came into being together; I and everything therein are One." Only through the equivalence of all things can one's real self fuse into the world; thus, the spiritual emancipation of humanity can be achieved.

Reading Comprehension.

Decide whether the statements are true (T) or false (F).

1. Zhuangzi (369 BC–286 BC), with his given name as Zhou, was a key figure of Confucianism following Laozi. _____
2. Zhuangzi believed that the "Tao" is the origin of everything in the universe. _____
3. The "Tao" Zhuangzi referred to is an omnipresent and finite concept in nature. _____
4. The experience of "xinzhai" means an attitude free from materialism and a complete unity with nature. _____
5. The philosophical basis of aloofness is realism. _____

The Hidden Meanings of *Yin* and *Yang*

You might have seen this symbol before, whether it's as a **temporary** tattoo or at a Chinese temple. It's called the *yin-yang* symbol. It comes from Taoism, a religion born in China and it has far more meaning than you probably realize. The *yin* is the dark swirl, and the *yang* is the light one, and each side has a dot of the opposite color, which gives a clue to the meaning of *yin* and *yang*. Everything contains the seed of its opposite.

Darth Vadar has the seed of goodness, and Luke has the potential to follow his father to the dark side. Like Luke and his father, *yin* and *yang* are not total opposites. They are relative to each other. Taoists believe that the universe is made up of energies, vibrations, and matter, which behave differently in different contexts. Something can be *yin* or *yang* depending on, well, depending on lots of things. So, while **wheat** that's growing is *yang*, when it's being reaped, it's *yin*.

A wave's crest is *yang*, and the trough is *yin*. Villages on the sunny side of a valley in China have names like Liuyang or Shiyang, but on the shady side, for example, of the Yangtze River Valley, there's Jiangyin. The **brake** is *yin* to the gas **pedal's** *yang*. An eggshell is yang, and the egg inside is *yin*. Do you think you're getting it? *Yang* is harder, stronger, brighter, and faster, but one can turn into the other or are two sides of the same coin. The sunbeams are *yang* in **comparison** to the shadows. The pitch is *yang*, and the catch is *yin*. The *yang* starts an action, and the *yin* receives it, and completes it. *Yin* is the inside space of a cup; it wouldn't be a cup without it. *Yang* is the cup. The coffee's heat, however, is *yang*, and its blackness is *yin*. *Yang* goes berserk sometimes, but there are some very powerful *yin*s, too, if they don't quite go berserk. *Yin* is the darker swirl, the female, but there is a white dot in it. And *yang* is the lighter, the male, but it has a black dot. Water flowing calmly in a river is *yin*, but when it goes over the waterfall, it's very *yang*. Toothpicks are *yin* compared with a telephone **pole**. The back of a person is more *yang* than the front. The top of a person is the *yang* end.

Taoism teaches that there is a power in the universe. It's higher, deeper, and truer than any other force. They call it the Tao. It means the way. The Tao has two sides. Unlike other religions where the higher power is all good, and perhaps has an all-evil **rival**, Taoism teaches that we need to learn from both *yin* and *yang*. And unlike religions with gods that are personal, the higher power in Taoism is not.

Taoists believe that living in **harmony** with the way,

a person will not have to fight against the universe's natural flow. So, for example, listen more, and argue less. Be ready to back up or undo something, and you will make even faster progress. Don't worry about being the best, be who you are. Live simply.

flexible [ˈfleksəbl]
adj. 灵活的

Complications take you away from the Tao. "The wise person is **flexible**," Taoists say. Learning to use the Tao is what Taoism is all about, and that's why you should know your *yin* from your *yang*.

Reading Comprehension.

Fill in the blanks according to the text.

1. *Yin-yang* symbol comes from _____, a religion born in China.

2. Taoists believe that the universe is made up of _____, _____, and _____, which behave differently in different contexts.

3. Water flowing calmly in a river is _____, but when it goes over the waterfall, it's very *yang*.

4. Unlike other religions where the higher power is all good, and perhaps has an all-evil rival, Taoism teaches that we need to learn from both _____ and _____.

5. Taoists believe that living in _____ with the way, a person will not have to fight against the universe's natural flow.

Viewing

Watch a short video of **Aphorisms of Taoism** and work in groups to discuss the following questions.

- How do you understand "When the student is ready, the teacher will appear"?
- Why did Laozi say Manifest plainness, embrace simplicity, reduce selfishness, have few desires（见素抱朴，少私寡欲）?
- "A journey of thousand miles begins with a single step." What is your understanding of the realization of the Chinese dream?
- Please talk about the influence of Taoism on Chinese culture combined with those aphorisms.

Appreciation

Excerpts from *The Classic of the Virtue of the Tao* (*Daodejing*)

Chapter 8   WATER

The best of men is like water;
Water benefits all things
And does not compete with them.
It dwells in (the lowly) places that all disdain
Wherein it comes near to the Tao.

In his dwelling, (the Sage) loves the (lowly) earth;
In his heart, he loves what is profound;

In his relations with others, he loves kindness;

In his words, he loves sincerity;

In government, he loves peace;

In business affairs, he loves ability;

In his actions, he loves choosing the right time.

It is because he does not contend

That he is without reproach.

Chapter 25 THE FOUR ETERNAL MODELS

Before the Heaven and Earth existed

There was something nebulous:

Silent, isolated,

Standing alone, changing not,

Eternally revolving without fail,

Worthy to be the Mother of All Things.

I do not know its name

And address it as Tao.

If forced to give it a name,

I shall call it "Great".

Being great implies reaching out in space,

Reaching out in space implies far-reaching,

Far-reaching implies reversion to the original point.

Therefore: Tao is Great,

The Heaven is great,

The Earth is great,

The King is also great.

These are the Great Four in the universe,

And the King is one of them.

Man models himself after the Earth;
The Earth models itself after Heaven;
The Heaven models itself after Tao;
Tao models itself after Nature.

Part V Practising

Translation.

Translate the following paragraphs into English or Chinese.

老子姓李名聃，是春秋时期伟大的哲学家、思想家，道家思想的创始人。他撰写的经典著作《道德经》，虽然只有五千多个字，却包含着朴素的辩证思想。他的作品充满着智慧，对后人的思想产生了深远的影响。老子反对物欲，重视精神生活，主张争取精神的自由和解放。在现代社会，他的哲学思想仍然具有重大的意义。

In the *Daodejing*, Laozi established a philosophy system centered on Dao. He refers Dao as invariable and constant Dao. He holds that Dao is the origin of the cosmos and that Dao is characterized by non-action, opposition, shapelessness, namelessness, obscurity, etc. Many Daoist principles have already been Chinese people's important ideals and norms and have exerted a profound influence on the development of Chinese culture.

Writing.

Please choose one of the following topics and write a composition of at least 100 words.

1. About Laozi.
2. What could you learn from *Daodejing*?

Chinese Painting

Learning Objectives

After learning this unit, you will be able to:
- learn the basic words and expressions, proper names, etc;
- try to introduce traditional Chinese painting in English;
- try to learn the history and stories about some famous traditional Chinese paintings.

Chinese painting, also known as brush painting or ink-wash painting, is one of the oldest art forms in the world. However, the varied styles, techniques, perspectives and symbolism of such paintings are often very different from most Western artworks. Also, the tools and media employed by the artists of traditional Chinese painting, such as inksticks, inkstones, rice paper and brushes, are unfamiliar to many Westerners. As a result, Chinese paintings, including many masterpieces, may seem mysterious to our readers. This series aims to explain the aesthetic concepts behind Chinese paintings and tell some interesting stories about their creation and their creators.

Chinese painting and calligraphy are almost always mentioned in the same breath, and both of them are favored by international travelers addicted to Chinese culture. Chinese painting is widely regarded as the highest form of traditional Chinese art and reflects profound philosophy.

Part 1 Lead-in

*Watch a short video of **Traditional Chinese Painting** and finish the following questions.*

1. Traditional Chinese Painting is mainly _____ ?
   A. oil painting   B. sketch
   C. wash and ink painting   D. watercolor
2. Tools and materials of traditional Chinese painting involve _____. (Multiple choice)
   A. writing brushes   B. ink
   C. rice paper   D. silk
3. It's very common that a Chinese painting is attached to _____.
   A. a character   B. a poem
   C. a name   D. a song

Decide whether the statements are true (T) or false (F).

1. Traditional Chinese painting often uses three dimensions or realism like western paintings. _____
2. If you understand traditional Chinese painting, you will have a better understanding of Chinese people. _____
3. The hardness or softness of brushes, paper absorbency and color determines the feature of Chinese painting. _____

Translate the following words into English.

Chinese	English	Chinese	English	Chinese	English
笔		诗		梅	
墨		书		兰	
纸		画		竹	
砚		印		菊	

Reading

Introduction to Chinese Painting

Chinese painting is one of the oldest continuous artistic traditions in the world. The materials used in Chinese painting, brush and ink on paper and silk, have determined its character and development over thousands of years. Derived from calligraphy, it is essentially a **linear** art, employing brushwork to **evoke** images and feelings. Once on paper, **brushstrokes** cannot be erased or corrected, so a painter must have a complete mental concept of the painting before even lifting the brush. Chinese painting is closely related to **Zen Buddhist** and Daoist ideals of total concentration in the act of the moment, and harmony between man and nature. The painter must work with speed, pitch, liveliness, confidence, and technical mastery, **infusing** spiritual energy into the brushstrokes. Chinese paintings do not attempt to **capture** the actual physical appearance of a subject, but rather its essential nature or character. Chinese paintings do not have a single perspective; every painting area is attractive to the eye. Landscapes are often painted from a viewpoint above the scene, so that many areas can be seen at once. In large scenes or landscapes, the eye is meant to travel along a visual path from one area to another.

There are three main subjects of Chinese painting: human figures, landscapes, and birds and flowers. Figure painting became highly developed during the Tang dynasty, and landscape painting reached its height during the Song

linear [ˈlɪniə(r)] a. 线的；直线的
evoke [ɪˈvəʊk] v. 引起，唤起
brushstroke [ˈbrʌʃɪzˈtrəʊk] n. 一笔，一画，绘画的技巧
Zen [zen] n. 禅，禅宗
Buddhist [ˈbʊdɪst] n. 佛教徒
infuse [ɪnˈfjuːz] vt. 灌输；鼓舞，激发
capture [ˈkæptʃə(r)] v. 俘房，占领；引起（注意、想象、兴趣）

dynasty. After Chinese painters were exposed to Western art during the nineteenth and twentieth centuries, they began to evolve new styles combining traditional Chinese painting with Western **impressionism** and perspective. The **aesthetics** of painting and calligraphy have significantly influenced the flowing lines and linear **motifs** that decorate Chinese **ritual bronzes**, Buddhist sculptures, **lacquerware**, porcelain, and **cloisonné enamel**.

1. Landscapes

2. Human Figures

3. Birds and Flowers

There are two main techniques in Chinese painting:

Meticulous—Gong-bi(工笔), often referred to as "court-style" painting, or "fine-line" painting. This style of painting incorporates delicate Chinese calligraphy strokes and close attention to detail. Fine brushes are first used to create an outline of the subject, and then the artist goes back with softer brushes to apply layers of color washes until the desired effect is achieved.

Artists always pay meticulous attention to every detail in their works.

meticulous
[mə'tɪkjələs] adj.
谨小慎微的；重视细节的；此处指工笔画

This is the *Monkey and Cats* of Yi Yuan-chi in Northern Song dynasty.

Fine details of the cat, including the eyes, tail, ears are clearly shown.

Freehand—Shui-mo(水墨)is loosely termed "watercolor" or "brush" painting. The Chinese character "mo" means ink and "shui" means water. This style is also referred to as "xie yi"(写意) or freehand style. This style emphasizes the **interpretive** aspect of brushwork and the shading of ink, and seeks to express the essence of the subject, rather than the details of its appearance. Only black ink and its shadings are used. Xie yi style has a freer, **unrestrained** look.

Development to 221 BC

Chinese painting originated around 4000 BC and developed over a period of more than six thousand years. In its **seminal** stages, Chinese painting was closely associated with other crafts such as pottery, jade carving, lacquerware and bronze casting. The earliest paintings were **ornamental**,

interpretive
[ɪnˈtɜːprɪtɪv]
adj. 作为说明的，解释的

unrestrained
[ˌʌnrɪˈstreɪnd]
adj. 不受抑制的，无拘束的

seminal [ˈsemɪnl]
adj. 有巨大影响的

ornamental
[ˌɔːnəˈmentl]
adj. 装饰的

not **representational**, consisting of patterns or designs rather than pictures. Stone Age pottery was painted with **spirals**, **zigzags**, dots, or animals. During the Warring States Period (475 BC–221 BC), artists began to represent the world around them.

Much of what we know of early Chinese figure painting comes from burial sites, where paintings were **preserved** on silk **banners**, lacquered objects, and tomb walls. Many early tomb paintings were meant to protect the dead or help their souls get to paradise. Others illustrated the teachings of the Chinese philosopher Confucius or showed scenes of daily life.

The earliest surviving examples of Chinese painting are fragments of painting on silk, paintings on stone, and painted lacquer items dated to the Warring States period. Painting from this era can be seen on an artistically **elaborate** lacquer **coffin** from the Baoshan Tomb (400 BC) An early painting on silk from the Western Han dynasty was found along with **exquisitely** decorated **funerary** items in a tomb at Mawangdui, Changsha, Hunan, China.

Reading Comprehension.

Fill in the blanks according to the text.

1. Chinese painting is derived from _____.
2. Chinese paintings do not attempt to capture _____ of a subject, but rather its _____.
3. There are three main subjects of Chinese painting: _____, _____ and _____.

4. In Chinese painting, the artists always pay meticulous attention to _____ in their works.
5. The style of freehand painting emphasizes _____ of the subject, rather than the details of its appearance.
6. Chinese painting has thousands of years and the earliest surviving examples of can be dated to _____.

Misty Bamboo on a Distant Mountain

Artist: Zheng Xie (1693−1765)
Year: Qing dynasty (1644−1911) Type: Ink on paper
Dimensions: 179.5 × 64.5 cm, 179.5 × 68 cm, 179.5 × 68 cm and 179.5 × 64.5 cm respectively
Location: Metropolitan Museum of Art in New York

Misty Bamboo on a Distant Mountain was painted by Zheng Xie, whose ink bamboo paintings became his signature. It is said that the renowned scholar Su Dongpo started the tradition of painting bamboo with only ink in the Song dynasty. And ink bamboo painting became so popular that it was listed as a separate category in "Painting Collection During Xuanhe Period", a **monograph** on Chinese painting compiled during the Song.

In Chinese art, particularly in traditional Chinese painting, four plants, namely the plum blossom, orchid, bamboo and chrysanthemum, are referred to the "Four Gentlemen", symbolizing **esteemed** characteristics and morals **pertaining** to gentlemen in Confucianism.

For instance, plum blossom usually blooms in winter or early spring. It doesn't compete with other flowers for beauty, but flourishes when other plants are depressed by cold weather. Therefore, it's a symbol of perseverance and self-control. Meanwhile, the orchid is regarded as noble and pure, and the chrysanthemum is dignified and **indomitable**.

The bamboo is unique though. The plant is admired for its straight stalks and green color even in winter. Since ancient times, Chinese scholars have seen bamboo as a symbol of being firm and **tenacious**. Moreover, as the bamboo stalk is hollow inside, it is also a symbol of modesty, honesty and uprightness, the most valued character traits endorsed by Confucius.

In Chinese painting, four plants, namely the plum blossom, orchid, bamboo and chrysanthemum, are not only favorite subjects, but also **revered** as the "Four Gentlemen", symbolizing esteemed traits and morals pertaining to gentlemen in Confucianism.

No wonder then that in the history of traditional Chinese painting, and especially in so-called **literati** painting, so many great artists left behind numerous paintings of the Four Gentlemen. Among them, Zheng Xie (1693−1765), commonly known by his **pseudonym** Zheng Banqiao, a celebrated painter of the Qing dynasty (1644−1911), is perhaps the most noteworthy.

Zheng was born into an **impoverished** scholar's family in Xinghua in east China's Jiangsu Province. Under his father's tutorship, young Zheng began to study writing, calligraphy and painting at the age of 8. The boy worked hard and showed exceptional talent in art.

When he grew up, Zheng successfully passed the imperial civil service examination first at the provincial level and then the highest level government exam in 1736. He then served **consecutively** as the **magistrate** of two small counties in Shandong Province, also in east China.

During his **tenure**, he made great efforts to help the poor, especially during natural disasters. He once even opened a government barn to help disaster **victims** before obtaining approval from his superior.

Also, because of his strong personality and uprightness, he **clashed** with his **venal** colleagues and attempted to push back against the **rampant** government corruption of his time. He tried to change all that, but failed. Finally, after 12 years, Zheng resigned from his government office in **disillusionment**.

Before that though, Zheng was once briefly appointed as the "official calligrapher and painter" for Emperor Qianlong during his inspection tour of Shandong because of his high reputation and outstanding achievement in art.

After his retirement, Zheng returned to Yangzhou, a prosperous, **bustling** business city close to his hometown. The city also boasted beautiful scenery and an artist-friendly atmosphere. In Zheng's time, it attracted many noted scholars and artists from various parts of the country.

In Yangzhou, Zheng made a living by selling his paintings and calligraphy. Because of his unique and **superb** style in both media, he soon became a key member of the Eight **Eccentrics** of Yangzhou, a group of great painters who advocated an expressive and individualist painting style and **shied** away from **orthodox** ideas.

Throughout his artistic career, Zheng painted three subjects almost exclusively, namely, bamboo, rock and orchid. He once called himself the **reincarnation** of the "all-season orchid, evergreen bamboo and everlasting rock".

His paintings usually feature rather simple compositions of bamboo, one or two slim stones and a couple of orchids. However, his paintings have long attracted viewers with their **vitality**, delicacy and gracefulness.

Zheng left behind quite a number of bamboo paintings, most of which are single-hanging scrolls. But one of them, called *Misty Bamboo on a Distant Mountain*, is different from the rest. This painting consists of four ink-on-paper hanging scrolls, measuring 179.5 × 64.5 cm, 179.5 × 68 cm, 179.5 × 68 cm and 179.5 × 64.5 cm, respectively.

Described as "monumental" by some art critics, this four-panel painting portrays, not just several, but a forest of bamboo standing along a mountain slope.

The painter uses dramatic and **intricate** ink wash **gradations**—from jet black to pale grey—to create an impression of field depth and the **veiling** effect of a dense mist.

Zheng's paintings are today hotly sought by collectors all around the world. In 2013, one of his bamboo paintings, *Ink Bamboo*, ink on paper, 169 × 80 cm hanging scroll, was **auctioned** off for 5.8 million yuan in Beijing. The four-panel *Misty Bamboo on a Distant Mountain* is now housed in the Metropolitan Museum of Art in New York.

Reading Comprehension.

Decide whether the statements are true (T) or false (F) according to the text.

1. During the Tang dynasty, ink bamboo painting became very popular and was listed as a separate category in the monograph. _____
2. Four plants in Chinese painting are called "Four Gentlemen", symbolizing the characteristics and morals of gentlemen in Christianism. _____
3. Zheng Banqiao was not only talented but exceptionally hard-working. _____
4. Plum blossom is a symbol of perseverance and nobility in Chinese painting. _____
5. As the bamboo stalk is hollow inside, bamboo is a symbol of modesty, honesty and uprightness. _____
6. Throughout his artistic career, Zheng painted mainly three subjects: bamboo, plum and orchid. Vitality, delicacy and gracefulness are the features of Zheng Xie's painting. _____
7. *Misty Bamboo on a Distant Mountain* consists of four ink-on-paper hanging scrolls. _____
8. Zheng's character is like bamboo in his painting works. _____
9. The Eight Eccentrics of Yangzhou shied away from orthodox ideas. _____

A Panorama of Rivers and Mountains

At the end of the Northern Song dynasty (960-1127), the whole China was facing a series of problems. The court was corrupted, the national military force was extremely weak, and the whole society was getting **unprecedentedly conservative**. In a word, the whole country was in severe crisis. However, in the same period art was developed at extremely high speed due to a series of art and cultural policies **initiated** by Emperor Huizong, who himself is a great artist. There are many great art works in this period,

unprecedentedly
[ʌnˈpresɪdentɪdlɪ]
adv. 空前地

conservative
[kənˈsɜːvətɪv]
adj. 保守的

initiate [ɪˈnɪʃɪeɪt]
vt. 开始，发起

and one of the most famous paintings is *A Panorama of Rivers and Mountains*. It was completed in 1113 when the artist, Wang Ximeng (王希孟), was only 18 years old. This painting was done on silk.

Wang Ximeng is one of the most famous artists of the Northern Song dynasty. At the age of ten, he started learning landscape painting, but soon he was sent to serve Emperor Huizong of the Song dynasty. Emperor Huizong believed Wang Ximeng was very talented and personally taught Wang Ximeng a lot of painting techniques. After a few months of study, Wang was offered the opportunity to visit and paint the famous mountains and great rivers in China. Gradually, he started to **specialize** in free-hand landscape painting and established his unique art style. Very soon his art achievements **surpassed** those of Zhang Zeduan (张择端), another famous artist in the development of Chinese landscape painting. The young Wang Ximeng became very ambitious and was determined to add some brilliant elements to the Chinese painting art. Probably this is the background of how he created this fantastic artwork at a such young age.

A Panorama of Rivers and Mountains is a scroll of 11.9 meters long and is divided into six parts. The painting depicts the greatness of mountains and rivers by using a lot of **Prussian blues**. Thanks to the mineral **pigments** used for this painting, this painting still looks very vivid and bright after almost 1,000 years. The artist applied traditional painting techniques and the style of Sui and Tang dynasties. The whole work is extremely magnificent and splendid.

---

specialize ['speʃəl,aɪz] vi. 专门从事，专攻

surpass [sə'pɑːs] vt. 超过；优于

prussian blues 普鲁士蓝（一种蓝色颜料）

pigment ['pɪgmənt] n. 颜料，色料

The waterfall flows gently down the mountain cliff; the fisherman drifts his boat gently on the lake; children are playing happily on the grass. In fact, if you look at the painting carefully, there are a lot of fine details. There are well-proportioned houses, quiet fishing villages and ancient long bridges and so on. Applied with fine pigments, the whole work is not only well-structured, but also very vivid and colorful. For example, the colors mostly used for this painting are: **azurite** blue, **malachite** green, pearl white and black.

  This painting is definitely a milestone in the development of landscape painting in Chinese art history. Using the special Chinese **seals** in this painting, China Post designed and published a set of nice stamps in 2017. Although Wang Ximeng died when he was only 23 years old, his art works are considered to play an important part in Chinese art.

azurite ['æʒuraɪt] *n.* 石青，蓝铜矿；蓝色染料

malachite ['mæləkaɪt] *n.* 孔雀石

seal [si:l] *n.* 印章

Reading Comprehension.

Choose the best answer according to the text.

1. Which emperor reigned when *A Panorama of Rivers and Mountains* was created?

    A. Song Huizong

    B. Song Renzong

2. The most famous painting, *A Panorama of Rivers and Mountains* was completed on _____ by _____, _____ years old at that time.

    A. cloth; Zhang Zeduan; 23

    B. silk; Wang Ximeng; 18

3. Why does the painting *A Panorama of Rivers and Mountains* still look very vivid and bright after almost 1,000 years?

   A. Because it's well preserved.

   B. Because the mineral pigments used in the painting.

4. The whole work is extremely magnificent and splendid and the artist applied traditional painting techniques and style of _____ dynasties.

   A. Tang and Song

   B. Sui and Tang

5. *A Panorama of Rivers and Mountains* is a scroll of _____ meters long and is divided into _____ parts.

   A. 11.9; 6

   B. 22.3; 8

Part III Viewing

Chinese Ink Painting

Watch a short video of **Chinese Ink Painting** and discuss the following questions.

- What are the features of Chinese ink painting?
- What philosophy does Chinese ink painting reflect?
- Why has Chinese ink painting become the main form of literati painting?
- What other preparation does the painting art need except for the painting skill?
- What are the differences between Eastern painting and Western painting?

Appreciation

Famous Chinese Paintings

Riverside Scene at Qingming Festival (《清明上河图》)

Riverside Scene at Qingming Festival is a panoramic painting by Zhang Zeduan, an artist in the Northern Song dynasty. It is the only existing masterpiece from Zhang, and has been collected by the Palace Museum in Beijing as a national treasure.

The hand scroll painting is 528.7 cm long and 24.8 cm wide. It provides a window into the period's economic activities in urban and rural areas, and captures the daily life of people of all ranks in the capital city of Bianjing (today's Kaifeng, Henan Province) during Qingming Festival in the Northern Song dynasty. It is an important historical reference material for the study of the city then as well as the life of its residents.

The painting is composed of three parts: spring in the rural area, busy Bianhe River ports, and prosperous city streets. The painting is also known for its geometrically accurate images of a variety of natural elements and architectures, boats and bridges, market place and stores, people and scenery. Over 550 people in different clothes, expressions and postures are shown in the painting. It is often considered to be the most renowned work among all Chinese paintings, and it has been called "China's *Mona Lisa*".

Nymph of the Luo River (《洛神赋图》)

Nymph of the Luo River by Gu Kaizhi of the Eastern Jin dynasty (317–420) illustrates a romantic poem by Cao Zhi from the state of Wei during the Three Kingdoms period. The copy collected by the Palace Museum in Beijing is a facsimile of the original made during the Song dynasty (960–1279).

The narrative silk scroll depicts the meeting and the eventual separation of Cao Zhi and the *Nymph of the Luo River*; the art captures the tension through the composition of the figures, stones, trees and mountains. The painting is one of the most important Chinese artworks, representing the beginning of the development of Chinese landscape paintings.

Emperor Taizong Receiving the Tibetan Envoy （《步辇图》）

Emperor Taizong Receiving the Tibetan Envoy painter Yan Liben was one of the most revered Chinese figure painters in the early years of the Tang dynasty (618−907). The painting is a work of both historical and artistic value, collected by the Palace Museum in Beijing.

The painting is 129.6 cm long and 38.5 cm wide, drawn on the tough silk, depicting the friendly encounter between the Tang dynasty and Tubo in 641.

In the painting, the emperor sits on a sedan surrounded by maids holding fans and a canopy. He looks composed and peaceful. On the left, one person in red is the official in the royal court. The envoy stands aside formally and holds the emperor in awe. The last person is an interpreter.

Noble Ladies in Tang Dynasty (《唐宫仕女图》)

Noble Ladies in Tang Dynasty are a series of paintings drawn by Zhang Xuan and Zhou Fang, two of the most influential figure painters during the Tang dynasty (618−907), when the paintings of noble ladies became very popular.

The paintings depict the leisurely, lonely and peaceful life of the ladies at court, who are shown to be beautiful, dignified and graceful. Zhang Xuan was famous for integrating lifelikeness and casting a mood when painting life scenes of noble families. Zhou Fang was known for drawing full-figure court ladies with soft and bright colors.

The paintings are spread around in the collections of museums nationwide.

Five Oxen (《五牛图》)

Five Oxen is a painting by Han Huang, a prime minister in the Tang dynasty. The painting was lost during the occupation of Beijing by the Eight-Nation Alliance in 1900 and later recovered from a collector in Hong Kong during the early 1950s. Now it is stored in the Palace Museum in Beijing.

The painting is 139.8 cm long and 20.8 cm wide. The five oxen in varied postures and colors in the painting are drawn with thick, heavy and earthy brushstrokes. They are endowed with subtle human characteristics, delivering the spirit of the willingness to bear the burden of hard labor without complaints.

Most of the paintings recovered from ancient China are of flowers, birds and human figures. This painting is the only one with oxen as its subject that are represented so vividly, making the painting one of the best animal paintings in China's art history.

Han Xizai Gives a Night Banquet (《韩熙载夜宴图》)

Han Xizai Gives a Night Banquet is a scroll drawn by Gu Hongzhong, a painter in the Five Dynasties and Ten Kingdoms period (907−960). It is now housed in the Palace Museum in Beijing.

The main character Han Xizai in the painting was a high official in Southern Tang, but later attracted suspicion from Emperor Li Yu. To protect himself, Han pretended to withdraw from politics and become addicted to a befuddled life full of entertainment. Li sent Gu from the Imperial Academy to record Han's private life, leading Gu to produce this famous artwork.

This painting, depicting scenes of Han's banquet, narrates through five distinct sections: Han Xizai listens to the pipa (a Chinese instrument) with his guests; Han beats a drum for the dancers; Han takes a rest during the break; Han listens to the wind music; and the guests talk with the singers. There are more than 40 characters in the paintings, all of the lifelike figures with different expressions and postures. The painting was Gu's most well-known work, as well as one of the most outstanding artworks from the Five Dynasties and Ten Kingdoms period.

Dwelling in the Fuchun Mountains (《富春山居图》)

Dwelling in the Fuchun Mountains is the magnum opus and one of the few surviving works by the painter Huang Gongwang in the Yuan dynasty (1271–1368). Many consider him a member of the "four great masters of the Yuan". He spent his last years in the Fuchun Mountains near Hangzhou and completed this painting in 1350.

The painting was drawn in black ink on paper. It vividly portrays the beautiful landscape on the banks of the Fuchun River, rendering the mountains, trees, clouds and villages and capturing the essence of the natural scenes in Southern China. It is regarded as the best landscape ink painting in China's art history.

Unfortunately, the masterpiece was damaged by fire and split into two pieces in 1650. Today, the first piece, 51.4 cm long and 31.8 cm wide, is kept in the Zhejiang Provincial Museum in Hangzhou, while the second piece, 636.9 cm long and 33 cm wide, is kept in the Taipei Palace Museum.

Spring Morning in the Han Palace (《汉宫春晓图》)

Spring Morning in the Han Palace was drawn by Qiu Ying, who specialized in the gongbi brush technique. He was regarded as one of the Four Great Masters of the Ming dynasty (1368－1644).

Qiu's use of the brush was meticulous and refined, and his depictions of landscapes and figures were orderly and well-proportioned. In addition to his paintings being elegant and refined, they are also quite decorative.

This particular painting is 574.1 cm long and 30.6 cm wide. This hand scroll work is a representation of various daily activities in the palace in the early spring, such as enjoying the zither, watering and arranging flowers, and playing chess. There are 115 characters in the painting, most of them concubines. There are also imperial children, eunuchs and painters. The painting is rendered with crisp brushwork and vivid colors. Trees and rocks decorate and punctuate the garden scenery of the lavish palace architecture.

One Hundred Horses（《百骏图》）

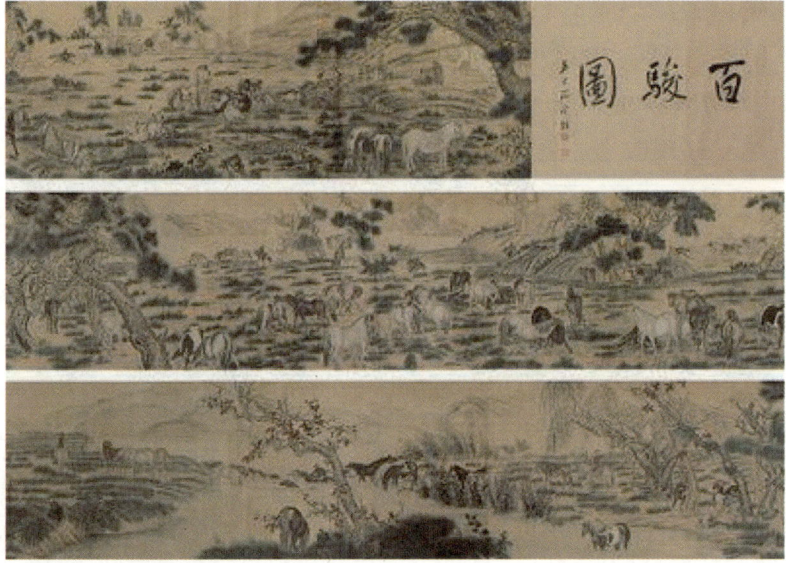

One Hundred Horses was drawn by Lang Shining in Qing dynasty (1644−1911). Lang was a missionary from Italy with the birth name Giuseppe Castiglione. Working as a court painter in China for over 50 years, his talent in painting was regarded highly by Chinese emperors Kangxi, Yongzheng and Qianlong. He helped to create a hybrid style that combined the Western realism with traditional Chinese composition and brushwork.

Lang was skilled at painting horses, and *One Hundred Horses* is one of his representative works. This paper painting, 813 cm long and 102 cm wide, captures 100 horses in various postures. They are kneeling, standing, eating and running on the grassland, staying alone and among groups. The artwork is now preserved in the Taipei Palace Museum.

Practising

Translation.

Translate the following passages into English or Chinese.

国画是中国文化遗产的重要组成部分。不同于西方画,它是用毛笔和墨汁在宣纸上作画的。精通这门艺术需要不断重复地练习,需要控制好毛笔,需要对宣纸和墨汁有一定的认识。绘画前,画家必须在脑海里有一个草图并根据他的想象力和经验进行绘画。许多中国画家既是诗人,又是书法家。他们经常会在自己的画上亲手添加诗作。

Qi Baishi was one of the most well-known contemporary Chinese painters. Born in a peasant family, Qi became a carpenter at 14, and it was largely through his own efforts that he became adept at the art of poetry, calligraphy, painting, etc. The subjects of his paintings include almost everything—animals, scenery, figures, vegetables, and so on. In his later years, many of his works depict mice, shrimps, or birds. Qi Baishi is particularly known for painting shrimps.

He theorized that "paintings must be something between likeness and unlikeness". His prodigious output reflects a diversity of interests and experience, generally focusing on small things of the world rather than the large landscape. Shrimps, fish, crabs, frogs, insects, and peaches were his favorite subjects. Using heavy ink, bright colors, and vigorous strokes, he created works of a fresh and lively style that expressed his love of nature and life.

Writing.

For this part, you are allowed to write *a letter to a foreign friend who wants to learn Chinese painting.* You should write at least 120 words but no more than 180 words.

Unit 5

Chinese Opera

Learning Objectives

○○○ After learning this unit, you will be able to:
- learn the basic words and expressions, proper names, etc;
- try to introduce Chinese Peking Opera in English;
- trace sources of Peking Opera.

China boasts more than 360 regional styles of opera. These ancient forms of drama are still active in China's stages today. A regional opera is usually popular in several provinces, while one province enjoys several local operas. Known as the national opera of China, Peking (Beijing) Opera is the most influential and representative of all the operas in China, and one of the three main theatrical systems in the world.

Peking Opera is a blend of music, dance, art, acrobatics, and martial arts. With its beautiful paintings, exquisite costumes, and graceful gestures, Peking Opera has developed into a comprehensive art system. Filled with many aspects of Chinese culture, Peking Opera presents the audience with an encyclopedia of Chinese culture.

 **Lead-in**

Watch a short video and try to remember some keywords on **Peking Opera.**

Watch a short video of **Peking Opera** and fill in the following blanks.

1. Peking Opera is a _____ form of Chinese _____ art, which combines the music of Chinese _____, singing, _____ dancing and _____.
2. Today, it is regarded as one of China's cultural _____.
3. There are four main characters in Peking Opera: _____, _____, _____, _____. Each character has a different age, _____ and social _____.
4. The masks in Peking Opera represent the different characteristics of the person on stage. Red signifies _____, intelligence and _____. Purple masks suggest _____ and sophistication. The black mask is regarded as _____. Whereas the green mask implies _____ and the yellow _____. The white mask actually stands for _____.
5. Peking Opera is a _____ art, and therefore not as straightforward as films and plays.

 Part II Reading

Peking Opera

Chinese opera, along with Greek plays and Indian **Sanskrit** opera, is one of the oldest dramatic art forms in the world. Watching a Chinese opera performance is a very rewarding experience, as the art incorporates music, song, dance, martial arts, acrobatics, and costume **artistry**, all rolled into one. To say Chinese opera performers are multi-talented is a bit of an understatement!

With its fascinating and artistic accompanying music, singing and costumes, the Peking Opera is China's national opera. Full of Chinese cultural facts, the opera presents the audience with an **encyclopedia** of Chinese culture, as well as unfolding stories, beautiful paintings, exquisite costumes, graceful gestures and martial arts. Since Peking Opera enjoys a higher reputation than other local operas, almost every province in China has more than one Peking Opera **troupe**. Opera is so popular among Chinese people, especially seniors, that even Peking Opera Month has been declared.

History and Development

Also known as xiqu, the art of Chinese opera reached **maturation** in the 13th-century Song dynasty but was already present in an earlier form called Canjun opera（参军戏）during the Later Zhao dynasty **circa** 319 to 351.

During the Tang dynasty, traditionally considered the greatest age for cultivating the arts, Emperor Xuanzong founded the Pear Garden, the first such academy of music, specifically to train up musicians, dancers, and performers. These artists formed what could be considered China's first opera troupe, though they mostly performed for the imperial family. This is why to this day, Chinese operatic professionals are still referred to as "Disciples of the Pear Garden".

From the Song to the Ming dynasties, other concepts such as rhyming schemes, specialized roles, and performing lyrics in the **vernacular** tongue were gradually assimilated into Chinese opera. Various **prefectures** in China would have their own versions of the art, but by the Qing dynasty, the best known was Beijing Opera, or Peking Opera.

Peking Opera has a 200-year-long history. Its main melodies originated from Xipi and Erhuang in Anhui and Hubei respectively and, over time, techniques from many other local operas were incorporated.

It is believed that Peking Opera gradually came into being after 1790 when the famous four Anhui Opera troupes came to Beijing. Peking Opera underwent fast development during the reign of Emperor Qianlong and the **notorious** Empress Dowager Cixi under the imperial patron, eventually becoming more accessible to the common people.

From the 1920s to the 1940s was the second flourishing period of Peking Opera. The symbol of this period was the emergence of lots of **sects** of the opera. The four most famous were "Mei" (Mei Lanfang 1884–1961), "Shang" (Shang Xiaoyun 1900–1976), "Cheng" (Cheng Yanqiu 1904–1958), and "Xun" (Xun Huisheng 1900–1968). Every sect had its groups of actors and actresses. Furthermore, they

---

vernacular
[vəˈnækjələ(r)]
n. 白话；行话

prefecture
[ˈpriːfektʃə(r)] n. 辖区

notorious
[nəʊˈtɔːriəs] adj. 臭名昭著的；臭名远扬的

sect [sekt] n. 宗派，教派

were extremely active on the stage in Beijing, Shanghai, and so on. The art of Beijing Opera was very popular at that time.

After the reform and opening-up policy, Beijing Opera had a new development. Especially as the traditional **quintessence** of China, Peking Opera got great support from the government.

Today, the Beijing Chang'an Opera House holds international competitions every year that attract many people from various countries. Peking Opera is also the reserved program for communication between Chinese and many foreign cultures.

Performance

In ancient times, Peking Opera was performed mostly on stage in the open air, teahouses or temple courtyards. Since the orchestra played loudly, the performers developed a piercing style of song that could be heard by everyone. The costumes were a garish collection of sharply contrasting colors to stand out on the dim stage illuminated only by oil lamps. Peking Opera is a harmonious combination of Grand Opera, ballet and acrobatics, consisting of dance, dialogue, monologues, martial arts and mime.

The Peking Opera band mainly consists of an orchestra and a percussion band. The former frequently accompanies peaceful scenes, while the latter provides the right atmosphere for battle scenes. The commonly used percussion instruments include castanets, drums, bells and **cymbals**. One person usually plays the castanets and

quintessence
［kwɪn'tesns］ *n.* 典范；精华；精髓

cymbal ['sɪmbl] *n.* 钹

drum **simultaneously**, which conducts the entire band. The orchestral instruments include the erhu, huqin, yueqin, sheng (reed pipe), pipa (lute) and other instruments. The band usually sits on the left side of the stage.

Peking Opera Masks

The main color in facial makeup symbolizes the **disposition** and destiny of the character. As one of the essential elements of Peking Opera, the masks can help the

audience better understand the opera. To put it simply, red indicates devotion, bravery and uprightness; black indicates either a rough and bold character or an impartial and selfless personality; blue represents **staunchness**, fierceness and **astuteness**; a green face tells the audience that the character is **impulsive** and violent and depicts surly **stubbornness**, **impetuosity** and a total lack of self-restraint; yellow signifies fierceness, ambition and cool-headedness; white suggests **treacherousness**, suspiciousness and **craftiness**; gold and silver colors are usually used for gods and spirits. The **archetypes** of masks were found in primitive society

simultaneously [ˌsɪməl'teɪnɪəsli] adv. 同时地

disposition [ˌdɪspə'zɪʃn] n. 性格；倾向；排列，布置

staunchness [stɔ:ntʃnəs] n. 坚强；忠诚；可靠

astuteness [ə'stju:tnəs] n. 敏锐；精明；机敏

impulsive [ɪm'pʌlsɪv] adj. 冲动的；任性的

stubbornness ['stʌbənnəs] n. 倔强，顽强

impetuosity [ɪmˌpetʃʊ'ɒsətɪ] n. 激烈，冲动，性急

treacherousness ['tretʃərəsnəs] n. 背信弃义；背叛；奸诈

craftiness ['krɑ:ftɪnəs] n. 狡猾，狡诈

archetype ['ɑ:kɪtaɪp] n. 典型

where people used masks to perform religious rituals.

The masks have three features: a combination of beauty and ugliness, an indication of the disposition of the character, and a fixed pattern for drawing. For different roles, the masks can vary a great deal. The makeup for Sheng and Dan can be simpler, while the makeup for Jing and Chou can be rather heavy, and for Jing, in particular, the pattern can be quite complex. The Peking Opera masks often refer to the makeup of the Jing. For the Chou, they only need to powder their noses so as to form the image of a clown.

Changing Faces

Peking Opera performers mainly have two types of facial decorations: masks and facial painting. The frequent on-stage changing of masks or facial makeup (without the audience noticing) is a special technique known as changing faces.

Changing faces is a difficult technique in **operatic** performance. It is considered to be a **stunt** that can only be mastered after extensive training. Face-changing is also a special technique used to exaggerate the inner feelings of characters, portray their dispositions, set off the atmosphere and improve effects. Facial changes expressing sudden changes in a character's feelings are done in four ways:

Blowing dust: The actor blows black dust hidden in his palm or close to his eyes, nose or beard, so that it blows back into his face.

Manipulating beard: Beard colors can be changed while

operatic [ˌɒpəˈrætɪk] *adj.* 歌剧的；歌剧风格的

stunt [stʌnt] *n.* 惊险动作，特技

the beard is being manipulated—from black to gray and finally to white—expressing anger or excitement.

Pulling-down masks: The actor can pull down a mask that has previously been hidden on top of his head, leaving his face red, green, blue or black to communicate happiness, hate, anger or sadness respectively.

Mop: The actor mops out the grease paint hidden in his sideburns or eyebrows, around his eyes and nose, to change his facial appearance.

Facial Painting

The three basic skills in painting Peking Opera masks are basing powder, coloring the face and drawing lines. Initially, the function of the masks is to suggest the disposition of the character by exaggerating different parts of the face. With the help of the masks, it is easier for the audience to follow the plot of the opera. Later, the masks were further refined and became an art with Chinese characteristics.

It is said that this special art derived from Chinese opera has different origins. But no matter what its origin, facial painting is worth appreciating for its artistic value. The paintings are representations of the characters' roles. For example, a red face usually depicts heroic bravery, uprightness and loyalty; a white face symbolizes a sinister, treacherous and guile character and a green face connotes surly stubbornness, impetuosity and lack of self-restraint. In addition, facial painting patterns reveal information about a character, as well. Essentially, the unique makeup allows characters on stage to reveal themselves voicelessly.

Xingtou

Peking Opera costumes are called Xingtou, or more popularly, Xifu in Chinese. The origins of Peking Opera costumes can be traced back to the mid-14th century when operatic precursors first began to experiment with large, ornate articles of clothing.

Since each dynasty in Chinese history had its own unique operatic costume, the number of costumes was too great for performers to master. Hence, artists and costume designers worked together to create costumes that would be unwieldy on stage and acceptable no matter when or where the action was supposed to take place. The stage image of some well-known historical figures, such as Guan Yu, Zhang Fei and Zhang Liang, were already fixed in the Ming dynasty (1368−1644).

Lavish costumes include:

★ Toukui, or Opera headdress: crown, helmet, hat and scarf

★ Costume (about 20 kinds): the ceremonial robe, or Mang; the informal robe, or Pei; and the armor, or Kao, for soldiers

★ Opera shoes and boots, or Xue in Chinese

Audiences can distinguish a character's sex and status at first glance by the type of headdress, robes, shoes and baldrics associated with the role.

---

lavish ['lævɪʃ] *adj.*
过分丰富的

Roles of Peking Opera

Over the past hundreds of years, the roles of Peking Opera have been simplified to today's Sheng, Dan, Jing and Chou, known as the four major roles in Peking Opera. The roles have the natural features of age and sex, as well as social status, and are artificially exaggerated by makeup, costume and gestures.

Sheng is the main male role in Peking Opera and can be divided into: civil and military; Laosheng (old man with a beard: dignified, polished, official, scholar), Xiaosheng (young man, shrill voice, young warrior, young man of society, stature, elaborate dress), Wusheng (acrobatic male, extremely agile and physically skilled).

Dan refers to any female role in Peking Opera and mainly consists: Qingyi (modest, virtuous), Huadan (flirtatious, playful), Guimendan (young, married girl), Daomadan (strong woman, female general), Wudan (female acrobat), Laodan (old woman).

repertoire
 ['repətwɑː(r)] n.
全部节目

entail [ɪnˈteɪl] v.
牵涉；使必要；势必造成

Jing is a painted-face male role. Depending on the **repertoire** of the particular troupe, he will play either primary or secondary roles. This type of role will **entail** a forceful character, so Jing must have a strong voice and be able to exaggerate gestures. Spectators are usually startled by the appearance of Jing. His facial colors symbolize the type of character: red is equal to good, while white is equal to treacherous, etc.

Chou is a male clown role. The Chou usually plays secondary roles in a troupe. Chou has the meaning "ugly" in

Chinese. This reflects the traditional belief that the clown's combination of ugliness and laughter could drive away evil spirits. Chou roles can be divided into Wen Chou, civilian roles such as merchants and **jailers**, and Wu Chou, minor military roles.

jailer [ˈdʒeɪlə(r)]
n. 〈过时〉监狱看守，狱卒

Reading Comprehension.

Decide whether the following statements true (T) or false (F).

1. Chinese operas, ancient Greek drama and Sanskrit drama are considered three ancient dramas in the world. _____
2. In the facial makeup, blue means uprightness and loyalty. _____
3. Xiaosheng, with artificial beards, presents the most common male character in Peking Opera. _____
4. Xiaosheng presents young generals skilled in martial arts. _____
5. Qingyi mostly stands for faithful wives, loving mothers, and pure women from the feudal society. _____
6. Jing is the most romantic and exaggerated role in Peking Opera and its actors usually have facial makeup. _____
7. Chou is the least important role in Peking Opera and often leaves little impression on the audience. _____

Kunqu Opera

Kunqu Opera first appeared in the late Yuan dynasty (1271-1368) some 600 years ago in the lower reaches of the Yangtze River. It was one of the earliest genres of drama in China and named for its birthplace, Kunshan, near the city of Suzhou in today's Jiangsu Province. During the reign of Emperor Jiajing in the Ming dynasty, Kunqu Opera came into being. As one of China's representative classic operas, Kunqu Opera nourished and nurtured many other operas, so it is called the mother of Chinese operas. The opera reached its heyday during the reign of Empero Qianlong in the Qing dynasty. Thanks to extensive exploration and recreation by its performers, it gradually developed into today's Kunqu. Besides, it became one of the three components of Peking Opera. Kunqu Opera was declared the World Intangible Cultural Heritage of Humanity by the United Nations Educational, Scientific and Cultural Organization (UNESCO) on May 18th, 2001 in Paris.

Characters of Kunqu Opera

Kunqu Opera is famous for its gentle and clear vocals, beautiful and refined tunes, and the perfect combination of dance and acrobatic performances. The music is much softer and the dialogue is more poetic and refined. The dance and movement of a role are gentle and closely connected with singing.

Musical Instruments

The musical instruments used in Kunqu Opera are distinguished from Beijing Opera. In order to match the poetry style of the play perfectly, the flute is widely used as the accompanying instrument instead of instruments with strings. Boasting for its time-honored history and all-around skills, Kunqu Opera is considered as the mother of many other traditional operas, influencing Beijing Opera. It was awarded as one of 19 "Masterpieces of Oral and Intangible Cultural Heritage of Humanity" by UNESCO in May 2001.

Development

In the early days, the songs were composed of many long and short lines. The singer sang the solo, and the orchestra, basically a **percussion** instrument, only came in at the end of each line.

Later, Kunqu music was reformed by famous musician Wei Liangfu, the forefather of Kunqu, in the mid-16th century. After his **refinement**, Kunqu became milder,

percussion
[pəˈkʌʃn] n.
〈音〉打击乐器
refinement
[rɪˈfaɪnmənt] n.
精炼，改良品；细微的改良

recitation
[ˌresɪ'teɪʃn] n.
朗诵

scores [skɔː(r)z]
n. 总谱；配乐

smoother and more graceful. Performers began to attach more importance to clear **recitation**, correct singing and pure tunes. The composers wrote the musical **scores** after working out the tunes, and the songs were written in seven-

character or ten-character lines. The accompaniment began to employ stringed instruments, bamboo flutes as well as drums and clappers.

Roles of Kunqu Opera

The roles of Kunqu are mainly divided into seven categories, including Sheng (male roles), Dan (female roles), Jing (painted face), Mo (middle-aged male roles), Chou (clowns), Wai and Tie, and each category has further subdivisions.

The Sheng roles, for example, have Laosheng (aged male roles), Wusheng (male warriors), and Xiaosheng (young male roles), each of which is further divided. Xiaosheng, the young male role, is divided into Daguansheng (big hat role), Xiaoguansheng (small hat role), Jinsheng (kerchief role), Giongsheng (pauper role) and Zhiweisheng (a warrior whose helmet decorated by a pheasant tail feather).

Stage Makeup of Kunqu Opera

The Kunqu style of stage makeup is mainly used for Jing and Chou roles, and occasionally for Sheng and Dan roles. The three predominant colors are red, white and black. The shades of blue, green, purple and gold are used to portray forest **brigands**, ghosts and demons.

brigand ['brɪgənd] n. 土匪，强盗

The same with Beijing Opera, the color red represents loyalty and justice, black conveys uprightness and straightforwardness, white signifies cunning and shrewdness, and yellow indicates a fierce, tough character. Most of the patterns and techniques of Beijing Opera facial makeup evolved from Kunqu.

Kunqu is of very great literary value for its rich traditional **repertoire**. Most of the themes of the stories of Kunqu Opera are about love romances. It seldom has too many military roles or acrobatic parts in a play. The representative works are *The Peony Pavilion*, *The Palace of Eternal Youth*, *Fifteen Strings of Cash* and so on.

repertoire ['repətwaː(r)] n. 全部节目

Reading Comprehension.

Choose the correct answer according to the text.

1. Which of the following Chinese traditional operas is the mother of Chinese operas?

A. Peking Opera. B. Huabu.
  C. Kunqu Opera. D. Zaju.
2. When did Kunqu come into being?
  A. Han dynasty. B. Yuan dynasty.
  C. Jin dynasty. D. Qing dynasty.
3. During whose reign, Kunqu Opera became prosperous?
  A. Emperor Qianlong. B. Empress Dowager Cixi.
  C. Emperor Jiajing. D. Emperor Kangxi.
4. _____ is widely used as musical instrument.
  A. Flute B. Pipa
  C. Drum D. Stringed instruments
5. Kunqu Opera was declared a World Intangible Cultural Heritage of Humanity by the UNESCO in _____.
  A. 2008 B. 2006
  C. 2003 D. 2001
6. _____ was called the forefather of Kunqu, a musician during the reign of Jiajing in the Ming dynasty.
  A. Liang Chenyu B. Wei Liangfu
  C. Li Kaixian D. Wang Jide
7. Most of the themes of the stories of Kunqu Opera are about _____.
  A. military events B. acrobatics
  C. love romances D. family
8. The Sheng roles of Qunqu Opera can be further divided into except _____.
  A. Xiaosheng B. Jinsheng
  C. Wusheng D. Laosheng

Part III Further Reading

Chinese Traditional Operas, History of Chinese Opera

There are five main types of Chinese Han opera: Beijing, Henan, Huangmei, Yue, and Cantonese Opera.

Beijing Opera

With almost two-hundred-year history, Beijing Opera is one of the most influential Han operas in China, and the quintessence of Chinese culture. It was listed on the UNESCO Intangible Cultural Heritage of Humanity List in 2010.

The History & Development of Beijing Opera

Beijing Opera developed from Anhui province traveling troupes, but is popular all over China now.

Because Beijing Opera entered the Imperial Court at an early stage, its development is different from other operas in that it is required to contain a broader theme, create more character types, and at the same time, tone down the Anhui style.

Costumes and Makeup of Beijing Opera

Beijing Opera features four main types of roles: Sheng, Dan, Jing and Chou.

The facial makeup uses a special method which emphasizes characteristics, whilst being an art form in itself, combining spiritual and artistic expression. Usually bat's, swallow's, or butterfly's wings are painted on eyebrows, eyes and cheeks, and nose and mouth are exaggerated to portray facial expressions.

The costumes of Beijing Opera have strong Chinese characteristics, and from the styles, audiences can identify the characters. The styles are divided into Dayi, Eryi, Sanyi and Yunjian.

The Music of Beijing Opera

The major instruments of Beijing Opera are the clappers（板）, single-leather drum（单皮鼓）, Chinese large gong（大锣）, jinghu（京胡）, jing erhu（京二胡）, yueqin（月琴）, and sanxian（三弦）.

Recommended Aria:
The Woman Prisoner (《女起解》)

The Woman Prisoner tells a story from the Ming dynasty (1368−1644), a woman named Su San being wrongly accused of killing her husband.

In this area, on the way to the execution site, she complains about her wrong treatment to an old man named Chonggong, whose duty is to escort the prisoners, and he consoles her.

The accompaniment instruments are plate, single-leather drum, Chinese large gong, jinghu, jing erhu, yueqin, and sanxian.

Recommended Opera:
Rapper Face (《说唱脸谱》)

Rapper Face is an opera that cleverly combines traditional Beijing Opera singing and rhythm with pop music, making it easy to sing.

The major instruments are the percussion clappers, single-leather drum, Chinese large gong, jinghu, jing erhu, yueqin, and sanxian.

Henan Opera

Henan Opera is the biggest regional opera in China, popular mainly in the Yellow River Basin and the Huai River Basin in central China.

Henan Opera can be divided into two styles: One mainly consists of singing and some dialogues with orchestral music, while the other focuses on acrobatic fighting with percussion music as accompaniment.

Costumes and Makeup of Henan Opera

Nowadays, the costumes of Henan Opera are similar to that of Beijing opera, and the actors also paint their faces.

The Music of Henan Opera

Henan Opera is famous for its singing style: the rhythm is distinctive and the lyrics are extremely colloquial. Every script describes a funny story or a legend, with scenes from the common people's life.

The major instruments of Henan Opera are erhu（二胡）, banhu（板胡）, pipa（琵琶）, suona（唢呐）, Chinese bamboo flute（笛子）, gong（锣）, drum（鼓）and guzheng（古筝）.

Now, some western instruments like violin, viola, cello, or even electronic organ can be used as well.

Recommended Aria:

Hua Mulan **(Excerpt)** （《花木兰（节选）》）

Hua Mulan was a legendary brave girl in the Southern and Northern Dynasties Period (420–589). This song praises Hua Mulan's saga of disguising herself as a man and joining the army in place of her father.

The accompaniment instruments are mainly banhu, erhu, pipa, dulcimer（扬琴）, guzheng, Chinese bamboo flute, suona, gong, drum, and cymbals（镲）.

Huangmei Opera

This style was formerly known as the Tea Picking Tune, and originated in Huangmei County, Hubei province. The themes are folk stories and legends, and it is popular with audiences for its liveliness and fresh regional style.

Costumes and Makeup of Huangmei Opera

The costumes of Huangmei Opera show strong Han characteristics, but heavy facial makeup is seldom used. Therefore, the performers look very natural and real.

The Music of Huangmei Opera

Huangmei Opera is famous for its natural and elegant style, simple and delicate singing and dancing make the characters lively and real.

The major accompaniment instruments are erhu, bangu（板鼓）, clappers, pipa, dulcimer, and Chinese bamboo flute.

Recommended Aria:
The Emperor's Female Son-in-Law（《女驸马》）

The Emperor's Female Son-in-Law tells the story of Feng Suzhen, who in order to avoid marrying a man she did not love, instead of her imprisoned betrothed, disguised as a man and took the imperial examination, achieving the best score.

Impressed, the Emperor betrothed his daughter to Feng, but on their wedding night, Feng confessed the situation to her. After many twists in the story, in the end Feng was saved, and married her fiancé.

The accompaniment instruments are mainly erhu, pipa, Chinese bamboo flute, sheng（笙）, cello, guzheng and so on.

Recommended Operas:
Silver Spear（《对花枪》）

Silver Spear is a newly-compiled historical play.

Luoyi, a sirdar in the Sui dynasty (581–618), bids farewell to his wife, Jiang Guizhi, because of the turmoil in the society. After several decades, Jiang Guizhi comes to find her husband from a great distance, and in the end, they recognize each other through competition in martial skills.

The accompaniment instruments are mainly erhu, pipa, Chinese bamboo flute, sheng, suona, and guzheng.

The Heavenly Maid and the Mortal (《夫妻双双把家还》)

The Heavenly Maid and the Mortal tells a love story of Dongyong and the Jade Emperor's seventh daughter.

Dongyong sold himself to slavery in order to be able to bury his father, which moved the Jade Emperor's seventh daughter (also called the Seventh Fairy). She descended to earth without permission, and married Dongyong under a locust tree.

She helps Dongyong to pay off his debt, shortening his slavery to 100 days. Before the couple can begin their life together, the Jade Emperor forces Seven Fairies to go back to heaven, so they have to part.

They are allowed to reunite only once a year, at the Qixi Festival—later known as the traditional Chinese Qixi, or Chinese Valentines Day.

The accompaniment instruments are erhu, pipa, Chinese bamboo flute, sheng, suona, and guzheng.

Yue Opera

Yue Opera is the second largest opera in China. In its heyday, there were many professional troupes in several areas of the country, but now it is mainly popular in Zhejiang, Shanghai, Jiangsu, Fujian, and other South Yangtze River areas.

The themes of Yue Opera have diverse styles and various formats, which results in a change in the performance form.

Costumes and Makeup of Yue Opera

The Yue Opera uses silks and satins as clothing materials, for their soft texture. Elegant, plain colors, and Mangpao (a kind of an embroidered robe with python as the pattern) are commonly used.

The Yue Opera tends to use soft and natural makeup, and the beautifying and painting methods make the characters look more vivid.

The Music of Yue Opera

The singing technique has its unique style, emphasizing the tone of voice and the way words are sung.

The major accompaniment instruments are erhu, bangu, plate, pipa, dulcimer, and Chinese bamboo flute.

Recommended Arias:
Sister Lin Falls from the Sky (《天上掉下个林妹妹》)

Sister Lin Falls from the Sky is a famous ballad from one of China's four great classic operas: *A Dream of Red Mansion*.

It tells the love story of the maid Lin Daiyu, who first meets Jia Baoyu just coming back from fulfilling a promise in the temple. The ballad describes their impressions of each other.

The accompaniment instruments are erhu, bangu, clappers, pipa, dulcimer, and Chinese bamboo flute.

***Bid Farewell in Eighteen Miles* (Excerpt from *Liang Shanbo and Zhu Yingtai*)** (《十八相送》(《梁山伯与祝英台》选段))

Bid Farewell in Eighteen Miles is a classic ballad of *Liang Shanbo and Zhu Yingtai* (also called *The Eastern Romeo and Juliet* or *Butterfly Lovers*).

It tells the story of Zhu Yingtai, disguising herself as a man to go to a private school, and making friends with Liang Shanbo, eventually falling in love with him. This aria expresses their love, and the feeling of being reluctant to part, as one sees the other off on the eighteen miles road.

The accompaniment instruments are erhu, bangu, plate, pipa, dulcimer,

Chinese bamboo flute and so on.

Cantonese Opera

Cantonese Opera, which originated in Foshan, is one of the local operas in Guangdong, as well as a Chinese Han Opera. It is widespread in Guangdong, Guangxi, Hong Kong and Macao.

As many Cantonese people have moved overseas from generation to generation, Cantonese Opera has become the world's most widely known Chinese Opera style.

The themes of Cantonese Opera are mostly adapted from classic novels, legends, folk literature, and local anecdotes, even from foreign novels or operas, which creates rich content in the plays, and makes people love it so much.

Costumes and Makeup of Cantonese Opera

The costumes of Cantonese Opera are made of silks and satins in bright colors. There are symbolic meanings to these colors; for example, yellow stands for respect, red for integrity, black for straightforwardness, white for graveness, and so on.

The early facial makeup for Cantonese Opera was mostly in a single color, but later the artists took the outlining techniques of Peking Opera's facial makeup as a reference, adding three-color facial makeup (red, black and white), five-color facial makeup (adding bright red and green), and golden facial makeup for mythic figures and other characters.

The Music of Cantonese Opera

Early instruments used in the opera were only erxian（二弦）, violin, yueqin（月琴）, xiaodi（萧笛）, three-stringed lute（三弦）, gong（锣）, cymbals, and bangu.

However, as many as 40 kinds of musical instruments are used in Cantonese Opera in its mature phase. These instruments can be divided into four categories: wind instruments, plucked instruments, bowed instruments, and percussion instruments.

Recommended Aria:
Parted Couple (《分飞燕》)

Parted Couple is a popular classical Cantonese duet; it describes the miserable feeling when lovers are apart.

The accompaniment instruments are guzheng, pipa, Beijing gong（京锣）, large wooden fish（大木鱼）, small wooden fish（小木鱼）, big gong（大锣）, cymbals, drum（大堂鼓）, and yueqin.

Part IV Viewing

The Beauty of Kunqu Opera

Watch a short video and discuss the following questions.

- Could you tell the differences and relations between Peking Opera and Qunqu Opera?
- What's your attitude toward "risk of disappearance"?

 Part V Practising

Translation.

Translate the following paragraphs into English or Chinese.

京剧是世界上最古老的戏剧艺术形式之一。从唐代起，京剧的表演者被称为"梨园弟子（theatrical performer）"。在清代，京剧在老百姓中也开始流行。表演是在茶馆、饭馆，甚至是在临时搭建的舞台上进行的。每个演员的脸上画着夸张的图案，代表每个人物的性格、角色和命运。这种技艺可能源于古代的宗教和舞蹈。熟悉京剧的观众可以通过观察人物的脸部描绘和服装来了解故事。

Peking Opera is a traditional art in China. It is a kind of Chinese Opera which was born when the Four Great Anhui Troupes came to Beijing in 1790, arose in the mid-19th century and was extremely popular in the Qing dynasty. Peking opera is widely regarded as one of the cultural treasures of China. Although it is called Beijing Opera, its origins are in the Chinese provinces of Anhui and Hubei. Peking Opera was originally staged for the court and came into the public later. Hundreds of years ago, as a new drama form, wherever it was performed, it would be warmly welcomed. Unfortunately, in the modern world, traditional operas including Peking Opera have to face the existential crisis, because they are not easily accepted by younger generations.

Writing.

Try to introduce one form of Chinese operas you like to the foreign students in our university. You should write at least 120 words.

Traditional Chinese Handicrafts

Learning Objectives

After leaning this unit, you will be able to:

- learn the basic words and expressions, proper names, etc;
- try to introduce Chinese handicrafts in English;
- trace sources of Chinese paper cutting, shadow play, etc;
- know about the Chinese world's intangible cultural heritages.

Some one said the handicrafts are productions of the culture. You can find a legend, an ancient story, a life attitude even the social trend in a folk handicraft. The handicraft industry at its very beginning marked the civilization, then kept evolving and finally appears gorgeous today.

Chinese handicrafts can be taken as one of the best cultural productions created by this innovative notion. There are countless artisans contribute themselves to this art field. You may think the norm abstract, intricate, or mysterious, but when you see close to some works, you would feel an undercurrent of power flowing in them.

Chinese people created brilliant handicrafts when they conquered the nature in more than thousands years. These multiform artworks are with the same age of Chinese history which is more than 5,000 years. It is the crystal of Chinese wisdom. In this vast land, various kinds of handicrafts tell people different regional legends as well as the unique culture only existed in China.

Lead-in

*Watch a short video of **Chinese Paper Cutting** and discuss the following questions.*

- Who invented paper-making 2,000 years ago?
- Why did Cai Lun improve the paper-making process 1,900 years ago?
- How did Chinese "Zhi" spread to the west?

Reading

Chinese Paper Cutting (I)

Facts About Chinese Paper Cutting

Paper cutting is an art of paper design, which is popular in nations around the world, such as China, Japan, Sweden, Mexico, and so on. People indeed divide paper cutting into the East school and the West school. Actually, paper cutting **originated** in China during the Northern dynasties (386–581). People used **scissors** or knives to produce wonderful decorative patterns of the paper by cutting and carving. Due to the economic development and cultural exchange of China in ancient times, paper cutting was spread to western countries in the 1600s. Gradually, paper cutting became a popular activity around the world. In 2009, Chinese paper-cutting art was declared the world **intangible heritage** by UNESCO.

History of Chinese Paper Cutting

Chinese paper cutting has 1,500 years of history. Since Cai Lun (?–121) improved paper in 105 AD, people started exploring more possibilities of paper by cutting and carving. The earliest product of Chinese paper cutting was **unearthed** at Flaming Mountains in Xinjiang by 2004, verified to be the cultural **relic** of the Northern dynasties. During the Tang dynasty (618–907), Chinese paper cutting entered into a period of **enormous** development. The **prominent** poet Du Fu (712–770) once wrote "暖汤濯我足，剪纸招

---

originate [əˈrɪdʒɪneɪt] v. 起源；发源

scissor [ˈsɪzə(r)] n. 剪刀

intangible [ɪnˈtændʒəbl] adj. 无形的

heritage [ˈherɪtɪdʒ] n. 遗产

unearth [ʌnˈɜːθ] vt. 发掘；挖掘

relic [ˈrelɪk] n. 遗物；遗迹

enormous [ɪˈnɔːməs] adj. 巨大的

prominent [ˈprɒmɪnənt] adj. 著名的；杰出的

我魂" to admire the fascination of Chinese paper cutting in his poem *Travelling at Pengya* (《彭衙行》). During the Southern Song dynasty (1127−1279), there appeared with **craftsmen** who made a living on paper cutting. Chinese paper cutting continued to **mature** in the Ming and Qing dynasties (1368−1911).

Moved into the modern era, Chinese paper cutting has **stagnated** for some time. But after President Mao **advocated innovation** in artistic creation in 1956, Chinese paper cutting **ushered** in a new era of development. Artists produced plenty of **contemporary** patterns of Chinese paper cutting, which enriched both the form and content of the Chinese folk **decoration** art.

craftsman ['krɑ:ftsmən] n. 工匠；手艺人

mature [mə'tʃʊə(r)] adj. 成熟的

stagnate [stæg'neɪt] vi. 停滞；不发展

advocate ['ædvəkeɪt] vt. 拥护；支持

innovation [ˌɪnə'veɪʃn] n. （新事物、思想或方法的）创造；创新

usher ['ʌʃə(r)] vt. 引入；引领

contemporary [kən'temprəri] adj. 当代的；现代的

decoration [ˌdekə'reɪʃn] n. 装饰；装饰品

Categories of Chinese Paper Cutting

Because of the huge regional disparity in China, paper cuttings are various in different places. They are usually fallen into the North School and the South School.

The North School: The style of the North school is concise and **straightforward**, focusing on the subjects. The North school consists of Shaanxi paper cutting, Shanxi paper cutting, Shandong paper cutting and Yuxian paper cutting in Hebei. Among the North school, Yuxian paper cutting is the most famous and special one since craftsmen will **carve** patterns instead of cutting on the rice paper. In 2006, Yuxian paper cutting was listed in the national intangible cultural heritage reserve. Except for Yuxian paper cutting, the other three **representative** northern paper cuttings are generally made by cutting with scissors.

The South School: Comparing with the North school, the South school concentrates on showing the details of the subjects, aiming to emphasize the **exquisite** skills of the craftsmen. There are Fujian cutting paper, Foshan cutting paper in Guangzhou, and Mianyang cutting paper in Hubei. Foshan cutting paper has existed since the Song dynasty (960−1279), having the longest history in the South school. In most cases, craftsmen in Foshan choose to make the flower-shaped paper cuttings to express their best wishes, while people in Mianyang and Fujian prefer to make animal-shaped paper cuttings.

Applications of Chinese Paper Cutting

With the 1,500 years that Chinese paper cutting has experienced, people have concluded three major applications of paper cuttings. Firstly, people use paper cuttings to decorate their windows, **cabinets**, and doors during holidays to increase the happy atmosphere. Secondly, paper cuttings are pasted on objects at weddings and funerals. Thirdly, people designed varieties of pretty patterns and printed them on clothes, sheets, and other **fabrics**.

cabinet
['kæbɪnət] n. 内阁；储藏柜；陈列柜

fabric ['fæbrɪk] n. 织物；布料

Reading Comprehension.

Choose the best answer according to the text.

1. When did paper cutting originate in China?

    A. Tang dynasty.

    B. Northern dynasties.

    C. Southern Song dynasty.

    D. Ming and Qing dynasties.

2. Why was paper cutting spread to western countries in the 1600s?

    A. Due to the economic development and cultural exchange of China in ancient times.

    B. Paper cutting has become a popular activity around the world.

    C. People divide paper cutting into the East school and the West school.

    D. Chinese paper-cutting art was declared the world's intangible heritage by UNESCO.

3. Which northern paper cutting is **NOT** made by cutting with scissors?

    A. Shaanxi paper cutting.   B. Shanxi paper cutting.

    C. Shandong paper cutting.   D. Yuxian paper cutting.

4. Which cutting paper has the longest history in the South school?

    A. Foshan cutting paper.   B. Fujian cutting paper.

    C. Mianyang cutting paper.   D. Jinhua cutting paper.

5. Which is not the major application of paper cutting?

    A. People use paper cuttings to decorate their windows, cabinets, and doors during holidays.

    B. Paper cuttings are pasted on objects at weddings and funerals.

    C. People designed varieties of pretty patterns and printed them on clothes, sheets, and other fabrics.

    D. Paper cuttings used to be used as patterns, especially for embroidery and lacquer works.

Work in groups to discuss the following questions.

- Why did paper cutting become a popular activity around the world gradually?
- What provided more possibilities for paper by cutting and carving?
- When did the craftsmen who made a living on paper cutting appear?
- What are the differences between the North school and the South school of paper cutting in China?
- Do you know other applications of paper cuttings?

Chinese Paper Cutting (II)

[A] Chinese paper cutting or "jianzhi" is the art of cutting paper designs, and the cut-outs are also used to **decorate** doors and windows, so they are sometimes called "chuang hua". Paper cutting has long been a symbol of eastern charm.

[B] There are **symmetrical** designs that are usually created by some folding and cutting. When **unfolded**, it forms a symmetrical design. Chinese cut-outs are normally symmetrical and are usually in an even number series of 2, 4, 24, etc.

[C] The oldest living paper cut-out is a symmetrical circle from the early 6th century found in Xinjiang, China. From the 7th to 13th century, paper cutting became popular, especially during Chinese festivals. The art spread to the rest of the world in the 14th century.

[D] Throughout the Qing dynasty many paper-cutting skills were developed. By the end of the Qing ruling, however, paper-cutting was once becoming weaker

decorate ['dekəreɪt]
v. 装饰；装潢

symmetrical [sɪ'metrɪkl] adj.
对称的

unfold [ʌn'fəʊld]
v. （使）展开；打开

because new art forms were being introduced. The People's Republic of China later tried to **revive** the art in the 1980s.

[E] Today, paper cut-outs are mainly **decorative**. They decorate walls, windows, doors, mirrors, lamps and lanterns in homes and are also used on presents or are given as gifts themselves. **Entrances** decorated with paper cut-outs are supposed to bring good luck. Paper cut-outs used to be used as patterns, especially for **embroidery**.

[F] There are two methods of **manufacture**: one is scissors, the other is knives. In the scissors method, several pieces of paper, up to eight, are tied together. The picture is then cut with sharp, pointed scissors. Knife cuttings are fashioned by putting several pieces of paper on a soft **foundation** made up of a mixture of oil and **ashes**. Skilled crafters can even cut out different drawings freely without stopping.

New Phrases	
be used to	被用作
even number	偶数
by the end of	到……结束时；在……尽头
be supposed to	应该

---

revive ［rɪ'vaɪv］ v. 使复苏

decorative ［'dekərətɪv］ adj. 装饰性的

entrance ［'entrəns］ n. 入口

embroidery ［ɪm'brɔɪdəri］ n. 绣花

manufacture ［ˌmænju'fæktʃə(r)］ n. 制造；制造业

foundation ［faʊn'deɪʃn］ n. 地基

ash ［æʃ］ n. 灰

Reading Comprehension.

Choose the best answer according to the text.

1. When can the existing oldest paper cutting date back to?

    A. About 1,500 years ago.

    B. About 1,600 years ago.

    C. About 1,400 years ago.

    D. About 600 years ago.

2. The underlined word "revive" in Paragraph D can be replaced by "_____".

    A. live longer
    B. bring it back
    C. copy it
    D. fix it

3. What does the last paragraph talk about?

    A. History.
    B. Tools.
    C. Uses.
    D. Process.

4. Which is true according to the passage?

    A. The oldest paper cut-out in history was found in Xinjiang, China.

    B. People believe entrances with paper cut-outs can bring good luck.

    C. Paper cut-outs used to be only used for embroidery.

    D. In the scissor method, more than eight pieces of paper are tied together.

5. What may be the best title for the text?

    A. Paper Cutting—the Eastern Charm.

    B. The History of Paper Cutting.

    C. An Introduction to Paper Cutting.

    D. Paper Cutting—Unbelievable Skilled Crafters.

In this section, you are going to read a passage with the following statements attached to it. Each statement contains information given in one of the paragraphs. Identify the paragraph from which the information is derived. You may choose a paragraph more than once. Each paragraph is marked with a letter.

1. Paper cutting was once becoming weaker because new art forms were being introduced by the end of the Qing dynasty. _____
2. Paper cuttings are mainly used as decoration nowadays. _____
3. Paper cutting has long been a symbol of Eastern charm. _____
4. Entrances decoration of paper cutting will bring good luck. _____
5. Chinese paper cuttings are normally symmetrical. _____
6. The People's Republic of China later tried to revive the art of paper cutting in the 1980s. _____
7. The oldest living paper cut-out was found in Xinjiang, China. _____

Work in groups to discuss the following questions.

- Please introduce paper cutting to a foreign friend in English.
- Try to explore one function of paper cutting with your team members.

Chinese Shadow Puppet Show

puppet ['pʌpɪt] *n.*
木偶；傀儡

Chinese shadow **puppet** show (play), also called Piying Show or Piying Xi in the Chinese language, is a traditional folk art, which traces back to the Western Han dynasty (206 BC– 25 AD). With puppet silhouettes made out of cow's leather or donkey hide, the shadow show figures of the Guanzhong area of Shaanxi Province are most represented in China. They were modeled after the stone **relief** patterns that originated in the Han dynasty. The academic-style painting of the Song dynasty (960−1279) and folk paper-cuts can also be found there. Today, Guanzhong play figures are popular with collectors as home decorations. Most tourists who visit Xi'an and Shaanxi are willing to buy them as souvenirs.

More than 2,000 years ago, a favorite **concubine** of Emperor Wu in the Han dynasty died of an illness. The emperor missed her so much that he lost his desire to **reign**. One day a minister saw children playing with dolls where the shadows on the floor were vivid. Inspired by this, the minister came upon an idea. He made a cotton puppet of the concubine and painted it. At nightfall, he invited the emperor to watch an **illuminated** puppet show behind a curtain. The emperor was delighted by it. This story was recorded in ancient books and is believed to be the origin of shadow puppetry.

Shadow puppet silhouettes were first made with paper sculpture and later used the hides of donkeys or oxen. This is why the Chinese name for shadow puppet silhouette is "pi ying", which means shadows of hides or leather. Shadow puppetry was very popular in the Tang and Song dynasties across China.

Shadow figureheads have a full profile, known as a "half face". Clowns and **villains** sometimes give half a profile, called "70% face", while fairies and Buddhas are shown with a full face. The Shadow figure's body is mostly 70%.

relief [rɪ'liːf] n. 浮雕

concubine ['kɒŋkjubaɪn] n. （旧社会时期的）妾，姨太太

reign [reɪn] vi. 统治；当政

illuminate [ɪ'luːmɪneɪt] vt. 照亮；照明；阐释

villain ['vɪlən] n. （小说、戏剧等中）反面人物，恶棍

Carving of shadow figures is particular. They require using a knife with ease and making turns smoothly. The hollowed-out facial outline, in particular, requires an exceptional skill in **craftsmanship** to make thin lines as "stretching wires", which are sharp and **translucent**. Body figures using **chisel** engraving have a variety of designs, including snowflake, character "王" shape, wealth and fortune, wintersweet, fish scale, pine needle and star eyes, etc. Leather silhouette coloring is often bright and transparent, black, red, yellow, or green. Music accompaniments are four-string and south string instrument, bowed instrument, four-string moon-shaped instrument, drum, gong, flute, hand **allegro** and horn. According to geographical localities each place has its own style and characteristic in shadow figure design, music and instrument.

To overcome their limit, shadow puppets use exaggeration and heavy dramatization. The faces and costumes of puppets are vivid and humorous. The flowery color, elegant sculpting and smooth lines make shadow puppets a work of art. A shadow puppet takes as many as 24 procedures and more than 3,000 cuts.

The figure of a shadow puppet show is from Chinese myths, legends and stories. Their designs follow traditional moral evaluation and aesthetics. The audience can tell a figure's character by seeing their mask. Like the masks in the Beijing Opera, a red mask represents uprightness, a black mask represents **fidelity**, and a white one is linked to **treachery**. The positive shadow figure has long, narrow eyes, a small mouth and a straight bridge on the nose. The negative one has small eyes, a **protruding** forehead and a **sagging** mouth. The clown has a circle around his eyes, projecting a humorous and frivolous air even before he performs any act.

protrude ['prəˈtruːd] *vi.* 突出；伸出，鼓出

sagging [ˈsæɡ,sɑːɡ] *vi.* 下垂

The rapid development of the modern economy in urban and rural areas, coupled with the growing influence of television and film culture, the traditional leather silhouette is almost precipitation into distinction nationwide except in a few regions in eastern Gansu, Shaanxi and Liaoning Province. Now only 200 leather silhouette troupes are still around, down from over 1,000 nationwide in the 1980s.

Reading Comprehension.

Choose the best answer according to the text.

1. Where has the most represented shadow show figures in China?
    A. 广东   B. 陕西
    C. 山西   D. 山东
2. Which is not mentioned as the fold arts that can be found in Guanzhong?
    A. Dragon boat carving.   B. Academic-style painting.
    C. Paper-cut.   D. Shadow puppet.
3. Who is shown with a half-profile in Shadow puppet?
    A. Fairies.   B. Buddha.
    C. Sacred god and goddess. D. Clowns and villains.
4. Which is not one of the factors that make shadow puppets a work of art?
    A. Flowery color.   B. Excellent sculpting.
    C. Heavy dramatization.   D. Smooth lines.
5. What does a black mask in Beijing Opera represent?
    A. Virtuousness.   B. Loyalty.
    C. Betray.   D. Integrity.

Enchanting Chinese Figurine

Chinese people love food made of flour, whether it be noodles, dumplings, or flatbread. Flour is a necessity in people's daily life. In the hands of skilled **artisans**, flour is molded and made into lovely figurines or animals to be enjoyed and played with hands, which brings unique pleasure. This art form is called dough figurine.

Dough figurines, also known as "**glutinous** rice figurines", are a traditional Chinese art form which uses wheat flour and glutinous rice flour as the main ingredients. They are popular all over China and are loved by both old and young.

Among the various art styles of dough figurines all over the country, Beijing's Dough Figurine Lang is a unique folk art, which is **imbued** with the rich history and customs of the capital city. The delicate and lovely Dough Figurine Lang handicrafts are storytellers of old and new Beijing.

The subject matter of Dough Figurine Lang is broad and focuses on depicting the real traditional life of Beijingers. The handicrafts not only have strong artistic and collection value, but can also provide an important reference for the study of old Beijing folk customs and folk handicrafts.

Most of the dough figurines are animals and characters from legends, historical stories, and local operas. The finished product is either put at the end of a thin stick, or on the table for display. The former is mostly for children to eat or play with, with simple forms and vivid decorations, while the latter are delicate pieces of artwork for display, crafted with **exquisite workmanship**. For this reason, during the making process, they are often mixed with additives to prevent them from cracking, being eaten by insects or growing moldy.

Dough figurines are mainly crafted by **itinerant** artists, who have mastered the skills to shape, model, and color the dough to make the figures look like what they want. They can transform the dough into a radiant artistic product in a short amount of time. This art, inherited and developed among the artists and the general public, embodies the **aesthetic** standards and ideals of the public, and provides the important subject matter for the study of Chinese folk history, customs, and art.

As one of the schools of dough sculpture art in Beijing, Dough Figurine Lang integrates drawing, sculpture, modeling, costume making, and other arts into one.

Dough Figurine Lang is made of wheat flour and

exquisite [ɪkˈskwɪzɪt] adj. 精致的，精美的

workmanship [ˈwɜːkmənʃɪp] n. 手艺，技艺，工艺

itinerant [aɪˈtɪnərənt] adj. 流动的，巡回的

aesthetic [iːsˈθɛtɪks] n. & adj. 美学；审美的，符合美学的

glutinous rice flour. During the making process, first, the flour is steamed, then **kneaded** into a dough and **pigments** are added to it. Then it is shaped into figures, animals, plants, or other images as desired.

As the dough is always sticky, artisans normally **moisten** their hands with wax before they begin to knead it. When making a human figure, the first step, "shaping" the face, is very important. Artisans need to shape a small piece of dough into a vivid and expressive face; every step throughout the process will be fined-tuned several times to make a face round and smooth and resemble human faces.

In the process of making dough figurines, the most commonly used tools are "pokers". They are either flat and pointed, good for cutting and carving, or round and smooth to roll the dough or make soft lines. In addition, there are also **tweezers**, small scissors, small combs, and other tools. Sometimes wool, feathers, threads, cotton, and other materials are used to make the whiskers, hair, crowns, and so on to increase the vitality of the face.

From the perspective of techniques, artisans first make a general shape by **pinching**, rubbing, and kneading the dough, then deal with details such as hands, feet, and facial expressions with a bamboo knife. At last, hair ornaments, dresses, and other minor parts will be added to complete the work.

Since dough figurines are generally small, attention and quick reflexes are highly required when making them. Whether it be making a nose, a mouth, sleeves, or a bead necklace, the artisan should hold the dough steadily and then work quickly with the small tools. A challenging part of making the figurines is when the time comes to paste the small parts onto the main body, as there is no chance to repair them after pasting them. So an appropriate proportion is needed in this delicate process. Otherwise the surface will not be smooth.

Dough figurines are not difficult to make. The true challenge lies in making them lifelike. Good handicrafts need the devotion of artisans from one generation to another.

Lang Jiaziyu, born in 1995, is the third-generation inheritor of Dough Figurine Lang. Influenced by his family, he cultivated an interest in making dough figurines during his childhood. His grandfather and aunt are superb artisans of this craft, and have had a great influence on him. Lang Jiaziyu looks a bit more fashionable than other folk artisans. Like many of his peers, he likes movies, cartoons, and memes. He has boldly introduced these elements into dough figurine art and has produced many popular and innovative characters. In the past, artisans mainly chose Monkey King, Guan Yu (an ancient general), and other classic icons to make their dough figurines. Now, in his skilled hands, pop culture icons such as figures based on Marvel comic characters, Slam Dunk figures, sneakers, Chinese mythological figure Nezha with smoky makeup, etc., are **resonating** with young people.

His innovation has won the admiration of many young people. Lang Jiaziyu has posted video tutorials online and received many comments asking for information about where to learn this craft. He is very motivated by people's love and recognition. Like most of the other intangible cultural heritage crafts in China, Dough Figurine Lang does not get as much attention from the public as it warrants. Many young people are unwilling to take the time to master a skill that does not make money, which as a result, has led to a decline in the number of those who are devoted to the craft.

In order to let more people know this heritage and understand the culture behind it, Lang Jiaziyu teaches the skill of making dough figurines at the invitation of some cultural institutions during which he presents the history and customs of Beijing related to it.

In 2018, Lang Jiaziyu was admitted to the School of Arts of Peking University for a master's degree. This experience will provide him with more opportunities to explore the great artistic values of this craft and also enable him to bring more value to this craft.

---

resonate
[ˈrezəneɪt] vi. 产生共鸣，发出回响

Reading Comprehension.

Fill in the blanks according to the text.

1. Dough figurines are a traditional Chinese art form which uses _____ flour and glutinous _____ flour as the main ingredients.
2. The handicrafts provide an important reference for the study of old Beijing folk _____ and folk _____ .
3. _____ are either flat and pointed, good for cutting and carving, or round and smooth to roll the dough or make soft lines.
4. In the past, artisans mainly chose _____ such as Monkey King, Guan Yu (an ancient general) and other to make their dough figurines. However, Lang Jiaziyu has produced many _____ characters.
5. Like most of the other _____ crafts in China, Dough Figurine Lang does not get as much attention from the public as it warrants.

Part III Further Reading

Chinese Knot

Chinese knot is a decorative handicraft that began as a folk art in Tang and Song dynasties, and became popular in Ming and Qing dynasties. It is distinctive for its complicated pattern woven separately from one piece of thread.

Development

Chinese people have known how to tie knots using cords ever since they began learned how to attach animal fur to their bodies to keep warm thousands of years ago. As civilization advanced, Chinese people used knots for more than just fastening and wrapping. Knots were also used to record the events, while others had ornamental functions. In Chinese, "knot" means reunion, peace, marriage, love, acquaintance and so on. Chinese knots are often used to express the above good wishes.

Types of Chinese Knots

The Chinese knots are named according to their different shapes, usages and origins. The treasure knot, for example, is with the appearance of "Yuanbao", the Chinese ancient golden ingot. And the button knot has the function as the button.

Each type of Chinese knots usually has a beautiful and auspicious name. The material of the thread can be the cotton, nylon and so on, and many of them are red. The exquisitely symmetrical knots that come in so many forms are the valuable cultural heritage of China.

In the ancient time, the knots are pulled tightly and sturdily together that can be used for binding or wrapping, which making them very practical. In addition, it is endowed with high decorative value by its complicated structure. Almost all basic Chinese knots are symmetrical, which has set certain technical limitations on the design and creation of new patterns. Traditionally, symmetry pattern suites the aesthetic standards of the Chinese people well. Moreover, the symmetrical designs are the most popular among Chinese people visually.

Making Processes

Making a Chinese knot involves three processes, naming tying knots, tightening and adding the finishing touches. Knot-tying methods are fixed, but the tightening can determine the degree of tension in a knot, the length of loops (ears) and the smoothness and orderliness of the lines. Thus, how well a Chinese knot has been tightened can demonstrate the skill and artistic merit of a knot artist. Finishing a knot means inlaying pearls or jade stones, starching the knot into certain patterns, or adding any other final touches. Besides the two-coin Knot, the Chinese knot is three dimensional in structure. It consists of two planes tied together leaving a hollow center. Such structure lends rigidity to the work as a whole and keeps its shape when hung on the wall. The hollow center also allows for the addition of precious stones, such as the jade.

Functions and Applications

The endless variations and elegant patterns of the Chinese knot, as well as the multitude of different materials that used have expanded the functions and widened the applications of the Chinese knot.

Jewelry, clothes, gift-wrapping and furniture can be accentuated with unique Chinese knot creations. The Chinese knot has been served as both the fixtures and decoration of palace halls and the daily implements of countryside households since long time ago. Large Chinese knot served as wall hangings have the same decorative value as fine paintings or photographs, and are perfectly suitable for decorating a parlor or study as well as the hall.

Chinese knot, with its classic elegance and ever-changing patterns, is both practical and ornamental, fully reflecting the grace of Chinese culture. With the economic and cultural global development, more Chinese people go abroad for business or study, which make Chinese knot widely spread in the world. It's an elaborate gift full of Chinese culture.

Reading Comprehension.

Read the text and decide whether the following statements are true (T) or false (F).

1. Chinese knot began as a folk art in Ming and Qing dynasties. _____
2. Chinese knot is made by only one piece of thread. _____
3. Chinese knots are often used to express reunion, peace, marriage, love, acquaintance and so on. _____
4. In the ancient time, the knots are endowed with high decorative value by its complicated structure. _____
5. Each type of Chinese knot usually has a beautiful and auspicious name. _____
6. Chinese knot is the reflection of Chinese culture, which has only decorative function nowadays. _____

7. Almost all basic Chinese knots are symmetrical, which are the most popular among Chinese people. _____
8. There are three processes to make the Chinese knot. _____
9. The Chinese knot is three dimensional in structure. _____
10. The hollow center means saving the thread and allowing for the addition of precious stones. _____

How China Became No.1 in World Intangible Cultural Heritage

Be it folk literature, traditional music and dance, medicine or painting, China, an ancient nation with 5,000 years of history, now has a total of 42 intangible cultural heritage after Tai Chi and the Wangchuan Ceremony were inscribed to the UNESCO List of Intangible Cultural Heritage.

As the protection of intangible cultural heritage is a task of all of humanity, China joined the Convention for the Safeguarding of the Intangible Cultural Heritage in 2004.

From 2005 to 2009, China carried out its first nationwide census of intangible cultural heritage, counting nearly 870,000 intangible cultural heritage resources, once again demonstrating the depth and width of the country's profound history.

Tai Chi Inscribed in 2020

Tai Chi, or taijiquan, is a traditional physical exercise in China that aims to bring the practicer health of body and peace of mind through its signature slow circular movements. Originating in Central China's Henan Province during the mid-17th century, it is now practiced by a wide range of people across various ages and ethnic groups throughout the country.

Acupuncture and Moxibustion of Traditional Chinese Medicine Inscribed in 2010

Acupuncture and moxibustion are forms of traditional Chinese medicine commonly practiced in China. In acupuncture, needles are applied to puncture and stimulate chosen points on one's body. For moxibustion, moxa cones are often placed on the skin to warm the chosen area.

Chinese Calligraphy Inscribed in 2009

Chinese calligraphy includes the five most well-known styles of script—

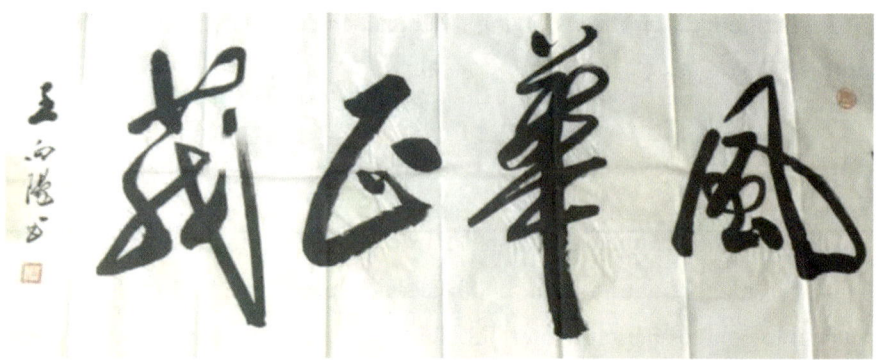

the Seal Script, Clerical Script, Regular Script, Cursive Script and Semi-Cursive Script. It can be seen as a form of art that embodies the essence of Chinese cultural aesthetics.

Dragon Boat Festival Inscribed in 2009

The Dragon Boat Festival is dedicated to the ancient patriotic poet Qu Yuan. It includes eating traditional foods such as glutinous rice dumplings and eggs. People also choose to bathe in herb water during the festival as well as to hang mugwort on their doors to avoid evil spirits.

Conservation Challenges

China has made huge contributions to the protection of intangible cultural heritage around the world since joining the Convention for the Safeguarding of the Intangible Cultural Heritage. Chinese government agencies, enterprises and communities have focused more on the discovery and conservation of intangible cultural heritage and more inheritors have appeared.

However, conservation work still faces challenges. Zhang Yiwu, a professor at Peking University, told the *Global Times* that these intangible cultural heritages need to be put into practice to remain vital.

"These intangible cultural heritages have some commercial value that are waiting to be developed. Cultural products related to them can serve society, which is also good for conservation", Zhang said.

He added that authorities should strengthen discovery and rescue efforts, as well as do more to introduce their cultural value to the public.

Part Listening and Speaking

News report.

New Words					
demonstrate	v.	证明	passion	n.	激情
promote	v.	促进；提升	calligraphy	n.	书法
intangible	adj.	无形的	woo	v.	追求；招致
celebrate	v.	庆祝	delicate	adj.	微妙的
thriving	adj.	繁荣的	detailed	adj.	详细的

In this section, you will hear a piece of news from VOA. Try to understand it and finish the following questions.

1. Where did Voyo Woo begin to study the art of Jianzhi?
   A. In the U.S.　　　　　　B. In southeastern China.
   C. Near Washington.　　　D. In college.
2. What did Voyo Woo get from paper cutting?
   A. Love.　　B. Passion.　　C. Fun and peace.　　D. Magic.
3. When did Ms. Woo come to the U.S.?
   A. 14 years ago.　　B. In 2008.　　C. Attend university.　　D. She was young.

4. Why does she like to know about Chinese art? Which is **NOT** the reason?

   A. It is very delicate.

   B. She likes the focus that it requires.

   C. Chinese art isn't for all people.

   D. Chinese art can resonate, and echo with people from other cultural backgrounds.

Listen again and decide whether the following statements are true (T) or false (F).

1. The first, earliest paper cutting was found in China 1,500 years ago. _____

2. Not all the students at Voyo Woo's school had to learn the art. _____

3. After finishing college, she became involved in an event to support and expand her understanding of Chinese paper cutting. _____

4. The promotion of paper cutting will lead to another thriving of this art form back in China. _____

5. Paper cutting represents Chinese cultural values, history and stories of people's lives. _____

Part V Viewing

Watch a short video and discuss the following questions.

- What are Chinese kites made of? Why?
- What are the innovations of kites today compared with traditional ones?
- Do you know the history of Chinese kites?
- Where are famous cities for kites in China?
- What are the cultural connotations of Chinese kites as for Chinese people?

Part VI Practising

Read the following passage and choose the correct word from the following answers.

A. social	G. focus
B. unique	H. emphasis
C. ideal	I. artists
D. realistic	J. urban
E. rural	K. broad
F. national	L. northern

Features of Chinese Paper Cutting

With a vast territory and multi-ethnic population, Chinese folk paper cutting bears distinct _____ and geographical features. In art style, _____ China is more straightforward, unconstraint, and _____ minded; while in the south, it is more exquisite and delicate, full of delight and witty.

From the creators, the _____ female folk artists use only a pair of scissors and paper to _____ their conceptual figures and color effect which surpass time and space; while male-dominant career artists make paper carvings with superb delicacy and graciousness in a more _____ style and art language. From the functionality in _____ life, paper cutting for embroidery patterns is given more _____ on the outline for decorativeness; while cave window decoration gives more delicacy to the inner pattern to let in light. In general art style, each artwork brings out a _____, personal touch of the author.

Translation.

Translate the following paragraphs into English or Chinese.

剪纸是中国民间艺术的一种独特形式，已有2000多年历史。剪纸很可能源于汉代，继纸张发明之后。从此，它在中国的许多地方得到了普及。剪纸用的材料和工具很简单：纸和剪刀。剪纸作品通常是用红纸做成的，因为红色在中国传统文化中与幸福相联。因此，在婚礼、春节等喜庆场合，红颜色的剪纸是门窗装饰的首选。

Clay figurine is one of the old folk arts in China. Its history can date back to the Neolithic Period（新石器时代）. With the clay as raw material, clay figurines are made manually into various images of humane, flowers, birds, insects and fish, among which the most famous are those by Clay Figurine Zhang. Delicate and vivid, his clay figurines are rich in regional customs. With the development of China's tourism industry, clay figurines have become popular travel souvenirs, favored by tourists from all over the world.

Writing.

Suppose your school is organizing a party with foreign teachers, and you are to write an introduction of Chinese paper cutting to them.

Unit 7

Chinese Embroidery

Learning Objectives

After learning this unit, you will be able to:
- learn the basic information about Chinese embroidery including words and expressions, proper names, etc;
- try to understand the history of Silk Road;
- know about the culture of "the Belt and Road".

Unit 7 Chinese Embroidery

Embroidery is the craft of decorating fabric or other materials using a needle to apply thread or yarn. Embroidery may also incorporate other materials, such as pearls or beads. In modern days, embroidery is usually seen on caps, hats, coats, blankets, dress shirts, denim, dresses, stockings, and golf shirts. Embroidery had a long history in China since the Neolithic age. Because of the quality of silk fiber, most Chinese fine embroideries are made of silk. After the opening of the Silk Route in the Han dynasty, silk production and trade flourished.

In the 14th century, Chinese silk embroidery production reached its high peak. Several major silk brocade styles had been developed, like Song Jin（宋锦 Song brocade）in Suzhou, Yun Jin（云锦 Cloud brocade）in Nanjing and Shu Jin（蜀锦 Shu brocade）in Sichuan. Today, most handwork has been replaced by machinery, but some very sophisticated production is still hand-made. Modern Chinese silk embroidery by hand is still common in southern China.

Part I Lead-in

*Watch a short video of **Chinese Embroidery** and discuss the following questions.*

- What is embroidery? Do you like it?
- What are freestyle embroidery and colored embroidery respectively?
- Why is embroidery often used in work clothes and heavily used textiles?
- Do you think embroidery is meditative too?
- If you can design your own embroidery motif, what will it be like?

Part II Reading

Silk

Although it was only one of many products traded, silk perhaps best encompasses the history of economic and cultural exchange across Eurasia along the Silk Road. The value of silk gave it particular appeal as a political and religious symbol, it was widely accepted as a currency, and it served as a medium for artistic exchange. The complex history of silk is both well-documented and in some ways poorly known.

When we speak of silk, in the first instance, we mean

that produced in China, where sometime probably in the fourth millennium BC, the Chinese learned the secret of unraveling the fine, rounded **filament** of the **cocoons** spun by a worm (Bombyx mori) which fed on the leaves of **mulberry** trees. There are other species of silkworms (for example, ones native to India), which produce a flatter filament or chew through the cocoon, leaving short fibers. It is the unbroken thread secreted by the mulberry worm which produces the finest fabrics. Silk is almost miraculous in its strength, lightweight and **insulating** characteristics. It provides a medium for writing and reproducing visual images; it is likely that the knowledge of silk processing led to the discovery of how to make paper from plant fibers, another Chinese invention. Early examples of silk fabric preserved in Chinese **burials** are decorated with "**auspicious** symbols" suggesting that the fabric had religious significance connecting humans with the natural and supernatural world.

Discoveries in Egyptian tombs indicate that some Chinese silk made its way to the **Mediterranean** world at least as early as 1000 BC. The routes of transmission presumably were the same, which developed more extensively in later centuries, overland across the heart of Asia or via the coastal trade around Southeast Asia and into the Indian Ocean. In most histories though, the real beginning of the Silk Road dates to the establishment of the Xiongnu **nomadic** empire on the northern borders of China around 200 BC and the development of a relationship between the Xiongnu and the Han Imperial court whereby large quantities of silk were shipped to the nomads to buy

filament
['fɪləmənt] n. 灯丝，丝状物

cocoon [kə'ku:n] n. 茧，保护层

mulberry
['mʌlbəri] n. 桑树，桑葚

insulate ['ɪnsjuleɪt] v. (使)隔热，(使)隔音，(使)绝缘

burial ['berɪəl] n. 埋葬，葬礼

auspicious
[ɔː'spɪʃəs] adj. 吉利的，吉祥的

Mediterranean
[ˌmedɪtə'reɪnɪən] adj. 地中海的

nomadic
[nəʊ'mædɪk] adj. 游牧的，游牧生活的，流浪的，漂泊的

peace along the frontiers and ensure the supply of horses and camels for the Chinese armies. This transmission of silk into Inner Asia established the pattern for later centuries, with the nomads receiving both finished garments, embroidered or woven with Chinese designs, and raw silk yarn and unfinished cloth.

Striking evidence of the Xiongnu's appreciation for silk has been uncovered in the royal burials in Mongolia, dating from the second and first century BC. The fabrics discovered there include woolen and silk embroidered with silk thread or decorated with silk **appliques**. Of particular interest is the fact that some of the embroideries depict faces of individuals who have distinctly "western" features, suggesting the possibility that even at this early stage in the history of the Silk Road, weavers from further west were employed by the Xiongnu in processing the "raw materials" imported from China. Such a pattern of the exchange of craftsmen involved in silk processing **recurs** throughout the history of the Silk Road. We cannot be certain who were the "westerners" depicted in the Noin-Ula embroidery, but there is substantial **archaeological** evidence even from some centuries earlier, documenting the presence in Inner Asia of people with "Indo-European" features.

The quantities of Chinese silk shipped on a regular basis to the nomads down through the centuries were substantial, often tens of thousands of **bolts** of silk or packages of silk floss annually. Possibly the peak of this exchange was reached in the Tang dynasty in the eighth and early ninth centuries, when as much as one-seventh

applique
[æˈpliːkeɪ] *n.* 缝饰，嵌花，贴花

recur [rɪˈkɜː(r)]
v. 重现，反复出现

archaeological
[ˌɑːkɪəˈlɒdʒɪkəl]
adj. 考古的，考古学的

bolt [bəʊlt] *n.*
一匹

of the government's annual tax revenue paid in silk was being used to obtain horses for the imperial army. The silk was important to the nomads, who acquired a taste for the luxury it provided. The process of building and maintaining a nomadic **confederacy** of the numerous tribes in the **steppe** was dependent in part on the ability of the nomadic ruler to distribute on a regular basis to his **allies** and relatives luxurious silks. Yet it seems quite clear that the quantities of silk sent to the nomads far exceeded their needs. The surplus has to have provided one of the important means for the nomads to acquire other goods they sought by trading the silk to those further west. Thus it is no coincidence that Roman sources from around the 100 BC begin to indicate a sizeable influx of silk into the Roman Empire, within a century or so following the initial agreements by which the Han supplied the Xiongnu with silk on an annual basis. By the 100 AD, Roman moralists complained that the taste for luxury (and for other luxuries imported from the east, such as spices) was bankrupting the empire.

confederacy [kən'fedərəsi] n. 联邦，联盟，同盟

steppe [step] n. 大草原

ally ['ælaɪ] n. 盟友，支持者

Reading Comprehension.

Choose the correct answer according to the text.

1. What is not the significance of silk in history?

    A. As a political and religious symbol.

    B. As an identity of the royal monarch.

    C. As money or cash.

    D. As a medium for artistic exchange.

2. Which characteristic of silk is not mentioned in Paragraph 2?

    A. Strength.   B. Lightweight.

C. Insulation.   D. Beauty.

3. When does the real beginning of the Silk Road date back to?

   A. Fourth millennium BC.   B. 1000 BC.

   C. 200 BC.   D. 100 AD.

4. What is the indication of the archaeological evidence in Mongolian burial?

   A. The presence of cross-race marriages between Mongolians and westerners.

   B. The presence in South Asia of people with "Indo-European" features.

   C. At this early stage in the history of the Silk Road, weavers from further east were employed by the Xiongnu.

   D. At this early stage in the history of the Silk Road, weavers from further west were employed by the Xiongnu.

5. How did the nomadic rulers deal with the extra silk?

   A. Traded them to Roman Empire.

   B. Distributed them among different tribes.

   C. Obtained horses for the imperial army.

   D. Broke the agreement with Roman moralists.

Four Major Styles

Chinese embroidery mainly has four major traditional styles: Su, Shu, Xiang, and Yue.

1. Su Embroidery

Su is the short name for Suzhou, a typical southern water town. Suzhou and everything from it reflects tranquility, refinement, and elegance. So does Su Embroidery. Embroidery with fish on one side and kitty on the other side is a representative of this style. Favored with the advantaged climate, Suzhou with its surrounding areas is suitable for raising silk and planting mulberry trees. As early as the Song dynasty, Su Embroidery was already well known for its elegance and vividness. In the Ming dynasty, influenced by the Wu

School of painting, it began to rival painting and calligraphy in its artistry. The wife of Sun Quan, King of Wu of the Three Kingdoms and Shen Shou of the Qing dynasty were both masters from this area. In history, Su Embroidery dominated the royal wardrobe and walls. Even today, it occupies a large share of the market in China as well as in the world.

2. **Shu Embroidery**

Originating from Shu, the short name for Sichuan, Shu Embroidery, influenced by its geographic environment and local customs, is characterized by a refined and brisk style. The earliest record of Shu Embroidery was during the Western Han dynasty. At that time, embroidered products were a luxury enjoyed only by the royal family and were strictly controlled by the government. During the Han dynasty and the Three Kingdoms, Shu Embroidery and Shu Brocade were exchanged for horses and used to settle debts.

In the Qing dynasty, Shu Embroidery entered the market and an industry was formed.

Workshops and governmental bureaus were fully devoted to it, promoting the development of the industry. It became more elegant and covered a wider range. From the paintings by masters, to patterns by designers, to landscapes, flowers and birds, dragons and phoenixes, tiles and ancient coins, it seemed all could be the topic of embroidery. Folk stories like the Eight Immortals Crossing the Sea, Kylin presenting a Son and other auspicious patterns such as magpie on plum and mandarin ducks playing on the water were also favorite topics. Patterns with strong local features were very popular among foreigners at that time. These local features included lotus and carp, bamboo forest and pandas. Some bought embroidered skirts and used them as curtains!

3. **Xiang Embroidery**

As an art from Hunan, it was a witness of the ancient Xiang (Hunan) and Chu (Hubei) cultures. It was a gift to the royal family during the Spring and Autumn Period. The most persuasive evidence is the articles unearthed in Mawangdui Han Tomb. Developing over two thousand years, Xiang Embroidery became a special branch of the local art. It gained popularity day by day. Besides the common topics seen in other styles, it absorbed elements from calligraphy, painting and inscription. Its uniqueness is that it is patterned after a painting draft, but is not limited by it. Perhaps because of this technique, a flower seems to send off fragrance, a bird seems to sing, a tiger seems to run, and a person seems to breathe.

4. **Yue Embroidery**

It, which encompasses the Embroidery of Guangzhou and Chaozhou, has the same origin as Li Brocade. People generally agree that it started from Tang dynasty since Lu Meiniang, who embroidered seven chapters of the Buddhist sutra, was from Guangdong. Portrait and flowers and birds are the most popular themes as the subtropical climate favors the area with abundant plants that are rarely seen in central China. In addition, it uses rich colors for strong contrast and a magnificent and bustling effect. Since Cantonese take to fortunes in an almost superstitious attitude, attaching a lucky implication to everything, red and green, and auspicious patterns are widely used. The most famous piece is *Hundreds of Birds Worshiping Phoenix*. Fish, lobsters, bergamots and lychees are also common patterns.

Reading Comprehension.

Decide whether the statements are true (T) or false (F) according to the text.

1. There are only four styles of Chinese embroidery. _____
2. Su Embroidery often has fish on one side and a cat on the other side. _____
3. In the Ming dynasty, Su Embroidery was still far behind its painting and

calligraphy. _____

4. During the Western Han dynasty, embroidered products were common and easy to buy. _____

5. The coverage of Shu Embroidery was very limited. _____

6. The most persuasive evidence of the royal family gift function is the articles unearthed in Mawangdui Han Tomb. _____

7. Xiang Embroidery is very vivid and lively. _____

8. Yue Embroidery has the same origin and pattern as Xiang Embroidery. _____

9. Red and green, and auspicious patterns are widely used because Cantonese take to fortunes in an almost superstitious attitude, attaching a lucky implication to everything. _____

10. All of the four embroidery styles developed due to the convenient conditions of raising mulberry worms. _____

Cheongsam

The cheongsam, also known as a qipao, is a close-fitting dress that originated in 1920s Shanghai. It quickly became a fashion phenomenon that was adopted by movie stars and schoolgirls alike. The history of this iconic garment reflects the rise of the modern Chinese woman in the 20th century. Shanghai, an active and vibrant port city with a large population of foreigners, was at the cutting edge of this fashion shift.

The cheongsam of the early 1920s had a looser cut than the cheongsam of today, with long, wide sleeves. It quickly became the regular outfit of urban women in metropolitan cities like Beijing, Shanghai and Hong Kong. As the garment evolved, traditional silks were replaced with cheaper, contemporary **textiles**. In terms of design,

textile [ˈtekstaɪl]
n. 纺织品；纺织业

traditional embroidered **floras** remained widespread, but **geometric** and art deco patterns also gained popularity.

Through the 1930s and 1940s, the cheongsam continued to change, **accentuating** the femininity and sexuality of the urban Chinese woman. The dress became more fitted and body-hugging, with some daring designs featuring side **slits** that reached up to the thigh. It became customary to pair the dress with high heels. Qipao itself has a feminine **silhouette** that flatters and **elongates** one's body. Furthermore, these Chinese-inspired elements like the intricate embroideries accentuate the elegance of the dress.

Later, the popularity of the cheongsam gradually declined, giving way to Western-style dresses, blouses, and suits. These mass-produced Western clothes were cheaper than handmade cheongsams, and by the middle of the 20th century, they no longer constituted everyday wear for most Chinese women. However, it remains a significant garment in the history of Chinese women's fashion. Cheongsam is the representative of Chinese women's clothing. It shows

flora [ˈflɔːrə] n. 植物群

geometric [dʒiːəˈmetrɪk] adj. 几何学的；似几何图形的

accentuate [əkˈsentʃueɪt] v. 着重；强调；使……突出

slit [slɪt] n. 狭缝；裂缝

silhouette [sɪluˈet] n.（人、事物的）形状；剪影；侧影

elongate [ˈiːlɒŋɡeɪt] v. 使……变长；伸长；拉长

women's gentleness, elegance, **virtuousness**, beauty and other **temperaments**. Cheongsam connects the past and the future, life and art, and is an elegant and noble beauty.

High-end cheongsam customization is a popular clothing industry, and there are precise regulations for every **stitch** and line, so the production cost is higher, and it can be more delicate and noble to wear. Today, I will introduce some of the production elements of cheongsam customization.

1. Version

A good cheongsam is fit first. Because of its strict close-fitting design, each cheongsam master will adjust the details of the version according to the customer's body shape after measuring, so that the clothes can fit to the greatest extent and can set off the owner's temperament. A well-fitting cheongsam can highlight a woman's beautiful figure **incisively** and vividly.

2. Fabric

The softness of the fabric directly affects the fit of the cheongsam to the body. Many cheongsam makers have said that almost any fabric can be used as a cheongsam. In terms of traditional fabrics, the harder ones are brocade, which can slightly conceal the imperfection of the figure, and are generally used in formal occasions or worn in Winter; silk fabrics are softer and can also be used in formal occasions, suitable for summer wear.

---

virtuousness
['vɜːrtʃuəsnɪs]
n. 美德

temperament
['temprəmənt]
n. 性情；气质；性格；秉性

stitch [stɪtʃ] *n.* 针脚

incisively
[ɪn'saɪsɪvlɪ] *adj.*
敏锐地；锐利地

3. Pattern

Today, cheongsam has begun to transform into daily clothing, but some important occasions still need some specific elements to reflect. For example, at weddings, brides usually wear styles with patterns such as phoenix, peony, lily, etc. If it is used for daily wear, young girls choose plain **plaid** to have a student atmosphere, and many people like the lotus pattern, which represents purity and elegance.

To distinguish the quality of cheongsam **craftsmanship**, the inspection of piping is a must-do homework. In addition to the outer piping, it is also necessary to check whether the inner lining piping is uniform and fine. There are strict regulations for hand-sewn **piping**. The hand feels softer. Too many stitches will cause the fabric to harden, and fewer stitches will make the process look rough.

plaid [plæd] *n.* 格子呢；毛呢

craftsmanship [ˈkrɑːftsmənʃɪp] *n.* 手艺；技艺；精工细作

piping [ˈpaɪpɪŋ] *n.* （衣服、靠垫等的）绲边

4. Cheongsam Embroidery

Embroidery is an important part of whether the cheongsam is of high quality. Embroidery craftsmanship in different regions of China has its own characteristics. The most well-known ones are Beijing Embroidery, Suzhou Embroidery, Hunan Embroidery, and Gu Embroidery. Among the cheongsam Embroidery techniques, the most common ones are Beijing Embroidery and Suzhou Embroidery.

We need to design the embroidery pattern of the cheongsam, and design different pattern effects according to the preferences and temperament of the owner of the clothes.

5. Buckle

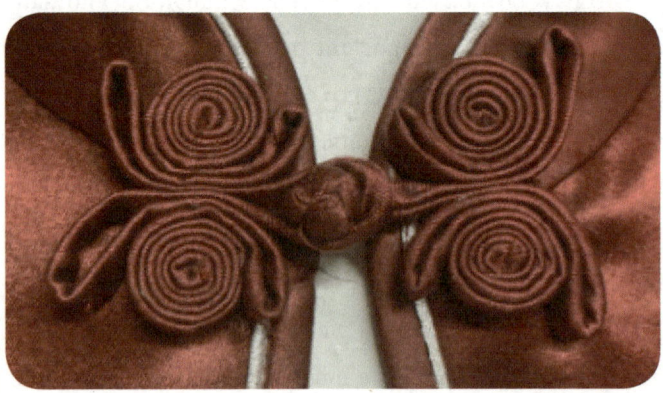

The button is the main form of connecting the placket, and its production process is an important part of showing the quality of the cheongsam, and it is also one of the unique symbols of traditional Chinese clothing. Traditional cheongsam buttons are used for the neckline, placket and slits of the cheongsam. For the convenience of wearing a modern cheongsam, the **placket** is mostly replaced by zippers, while the collar must have a button, which is practical and decorative. Although the buttons are small, the production process is even more complicated than sewing clothes. Chrysanthemum buttons, orchid buttons, etc., are common in plant patterns, and there are Fu, Lu, Shou, Xi series, as well as dragon, phoenix and other styles, mostly have auspicious meanings.

The buckle contains the unique cultural connotation of the Chinese nation. Speaking of the "pan buckle", its history is not long. It is developed from the ancient "knot". In the early Chinese clothing, in order to keep the clothes fit and warm without falling apart, it was necessary to rely

on belts and **ropes**, and when using them, buttons and knots were required. The styles of knots are very rich, there are knots for the function of binding clothes, and there are also knots for decorations that play a beautifying effect. At the same time, knots also represent various good and auspicious meanings in people's minds.

As a kind of clothing with great artistic beauty and historical **precipitation**, cheongsam is widely praised by the world. It highlights the beauty and elegance of women and **unleashes** a unique charm. If you want to be stylish, then you might as well make a cheongsam for yourself!

rope [rəup] n. 绳子；绳索

precipitation [prɪˌsɪpɪ'teɪʃn] n. 沉淀

unleash [ʌn'liːʃ] v. 发泄；突然释放

Reading Comprehension.

Read the text and fill in the blanks.

1. In the early 1920s, the cheongsam with a looser cut and long, wide sleeves quickly became the regular outfit of urban women in _____ cities.
2. Through the 1930s and 1940s, the cheongsam continued to change, accentuating the _____ and _____ of the urban Chinese woman.

3. Because of its strict _____ design, each cheongsam can fit to the greatest extent and can set off the owner's _____.
4. Embroidery craftsmanship in different regions of China has its own _____.
5. The collar must have a button, which is described as both _____ and _____.

Part III Viewing

Miao Embroidery

Watch a short video and discuss the following questions.

- What does Miao Embroidery originate?
- What are the features of Miao Embroidery?
- What are the differences between Miao Embroidery and the other four major embroideries in China?
- How could Miao Embroidery help to achieve the rural revitalization?
- How to protect our China's intangible cultural heritage like Miao Embroidery?

Part IV Further Reading

Origins and History

The history of silk begins in China-silkworms were domesticated as early as 5,000 years ago. Silk, in textile and embroidery form, was the main product transported along the ancient Chinese Silk Road. The production of silk thread and fabrics gave rise to the art of embroidery. Simple embroidery decoration was customarily worked on wool, linen, and hemp cloth as far back as the Neolithic (the last stage of the Stone Age) period.

The oldest embroidered product in China on record dates from Shang dynasty. It was not until later on, as the national economy developed, that embroidery entered the lives of the common people.

The Development of Chinese Embroidery

The Chinese art of embroidery attained a fairly high level in the dynasties of Qing and Han more than 2,000 years ago. Embroideries, silks and silk fabrics were the major commodities transported along the Silk Road. Historical records show that the official robes worn by monarchs and their subordinates more than 4,000 years ago were either painted or embroidered. Later, officials' uniforms were embroidered with silk dyed in cinnabar.

As early as the Western Han dynasty, embroidery had gradually become an art, and the famous embroiderers were accorded a special place in the history of fine arts. The most outstanding four major Chinese embroidery forms took shape in the middle of the 19th century.

Apart from their own distinctive characteristics, the commercialization of embroideries was another important cause for their emergence. Because of the market demand and their different places of origin, embroidered products became well-known indigenous commodities.

The Craftsmanship of Chinese Embroidery

Embroiderers usually split a hair-thin thread into 2 to 16 thinner threads. Different thread thicknesses are used for different parts of a subject in embroidery to create subtle shades, smooth color transitions, and a lifelike effect.

Few masters have the capability to apply a thinner line than 1/2 thin-line (i.e., 1/32 of silk thread), correspondingly, the price will be five or more times than the normal one.

A Window into Chinese Culture

Due to their connections with Chinese philosophy, aesthetics and history, the Chinese embroidery arts provide a fascinating window into traditional Chinese culture.

One of the best ways to understand China, Chinese culture and Chinese embroidery is to experience them for yourself. Starting from watching embroidery teaching videos is a great way to gain a deeper understanding of Chinese culture.

Part V Practising

Translation.

Translate the following paragraphs into English or Chinese.

刺绣（embroidery）是中国的民间传统手工艺之一，有超过两千年的历史。刺绣就是用针线在织物上绣上（embroider）各种装饰性的图案。中国刺绣与养蚕业（sericulture）紧密相连，中国是世界上最早使用蚕丝的国家。刺绣的用途主要包括生活和艺术装饰，如服装、床上用品（bedclothes）、台布和舞台装饰。刺绣在国外也享有很高的声誉，是中国文化艺术的杰出代表之一。

The cheongsam is a female dress with distinctive Chinese features and enjoys a growing popularity in the international world of high fashion. Easy to slip on and comfortable to wear, the cheongsam fits well the female Chinese figure. Its neck is high, collar closed, and its sleeves may be either short, medium or full length, depending on seasons and tastes. The dress is buttoned on the right side, with a loose chest and a fitting waist. The beauty of the cheongsam is that, made of different materials and to varying lengths, it can be worn either on casual or formal occasions. In either case, it creates an impression of simple and quiet charm, elegance and neatness.

Writing.

If your friend will be married soon, please recommend a Chinese cheongsam to her. You should write at least 120 words.

Chinese Kung Fu

Learning Objectives

After learning this unit, you will be able to:
- learn the basic theory of *Yin* and *Yang* in Chinese Kung Fu;
- try to introduce Chinese Kung Fu to foreigners and understand the spirit of Chinese Kung Fu;
- trace sources of Chinese Kung Fu.

Chinese Kung Fu (Martial Arts, popularly referred to as Gongfu or Wushu) is a series of fighting styles which has developed over a long historical period in China. Nowadays, it is regarded as a traditional sport gaining more and more popularity and even stands as a representative of Chinese culture. Styles including Shaolin, Tai Chi and Qigong have many followers worldwide. Some westerners think that all Chinese people are Kung Fu masters. That's not true, but this traditional heritage has its unique existence in modern times and left much influence on the locals' lifestyle.

Although being fighting styles, Kung Fu advocates virtue and peace, not aggression or violence. This has been the common value upheld by martial artists from generation to generation. With a number of movement sets, boxing styles, weapon skills and some fighting stunts, Kung Fu keeps its original function of self-defense. Now its value in body-building and fitness is also highly appreciated.

 Lead-in

*Watch a short video of **Kung Fu Panda** and discuss the following question.*

- Do you like *Kung Fu Panda*? Why?
- Are there any secrets of Chinese Kung Fu? What are they?
- Is there any philosophy you can learn from the film? What do you think of the philosophy or value of Chinese Kung Fu?
- Does this film accurately reflect the Chinese culture? What are they?
- How do you comment on *Kung Fu Panda*?

Complete the paragraphs with suitable words in the following.

A. profound   F. philosophy

B. connotations   G. offensive and defensive

C. outstanding   H. heritage

D. punches   I. evolved

E. balance   J. dynamic

When it comes to Chinese Kung Fu, people may think of the well-known movie *Kung Fu Panda* or the (1) _____ person Bruce Lee. Chinese Kung Fu, also known as Chinese martial arts, is a traditional Chinese sports event. Based on (2) _____ combat actions such as kicks, (3) _____, wrestling and so on, Chinese Kung Fu (4) _____ from the ways of human fighting and combat in ancient times. In addition to combat techniques, Chinese Kung Fu bases its ideological root upon Chinese (5) _____, an understanding of life and the universe. It has a long history and it is a valuable cultural (6) _____ of China. Chinese Kung Fu emphasizes a(an) (7) _____ between hardness and softness which presents the robust beauty and (8) _____ elegance of a person. The physical movements are (9) _____ on the outside, while the internal thoughts are static; the energy is fierce on the outside and quiet on the inside. It involves a variety of schools, different techniques, and cultural (10) _____. Nowadays, Chinese Kung Fu has entered universities and has spread all over the world.

Part II Reading

Yin Yang

The basic structure of YIN YANG CHI (Kung Fu martial art) is based on the theory of *yin* and *yang*, a pair of mutually complementary and interdependent forces that act continuously, without cessation, in this universe. Harmony is regarded as the basic principle of the world order, as a **cosmic** field of force in which *yin* and *yang* are eternally complimentary and eternally changing.

The figure shows the symbol of *yin* and *yang* are two **interlocking** parts of one whole. The ancient character of *yin*, the black part of the circle, is a drawing of clouds and hills. *Yin* can represent anything in the universe: negativeness, passiveness, gentleness, internal, insubstantiality, femaleness, moon, darkness, night, earth,

cosmic [ˈkɒzmɪk]
adj. 宇宙的

interlocking
[ɪntə(ː)ˈlɒkɪŋ]
adj. 联锁的

rest, flat, etc. The other complementary part of the circle is yang. The lower part of the character signifies **slanting** sunrays, while the upper part represents the sun. Yang can represent anything in the universe: positiveness, activeness, firmness, external, substantiality, maleness, sun, brightness, day, heaven, light, etc.

In the *yin-yang* symbol, there is a white spot on the black part and a black spot on the white part. This is illustrating the balance in life, for nothing can survive long by going to either extremes, be it pure *yin* (negativeness) or *yang* (positiveness). Extreme heat kills, as does extreme cold. No violent extremes endure. Nothing lasts but **sober** moderation. Notice that the stiffest tree most easily cracked, while the bamboo or willow survives by bending with the wind. Firmness without **pliancy** is like a barrel without water, and pliancy without firmness is like water without a barrel. In Kung Fu, *yang* should be concealed in *yin*, which is represented symbolically by the white spot on the black part, and *yin* in *yang*, which is represented symbolically by the black spot on the white part. A Kung Fu man, should be soft-yet not yielding; firm-yet not hard.

When the movement of *yin/yang* flows into extremes, the reaction sets in. For when *yang* goes to the extreme, it changed back to *yin* and vice versa, each being the cause and result of the other. For example, when one works to the extreme, he becomes tired and has to rest. (a transition from *yang* to *yin*). After resting, he can work again (a transition of *yin* back to *yang*). This **incessant** changing of *yin/yang* is always continuous.

Therefore, in Kung Fu one should be in harmony with, and not in opposition against, the force of one opponent.

Gentleness and firmness (*yin* & *yang*) are two interdependent and complementary forces in Yin Yang Chi Kung Fu, and the aim is the **attainment** and maintenance of perfect balance between these two forces.

Gentleness/Firmness is one inseparable force of one unceasing **interplay** of movement. If a person riding a bicycle wishes to go somewhere, for example, he can't pump on both **pedals** at the same time or not pump on them at all. In order to move forward, he pumps on one pedal while **simultaneously** releasing the other. So the movement of going forward requires this "oneness" of pumping and **releasing**. Pumping then is the result of releasing and vice versa, each being the cause of the other.

Firmness and gentleness in the art of Kung Fu are not **isolated**, but **coalescent**, and the same goes for the various movements such as attack and defense, expansion and contraction, pushing and pulling, etc.

Therefore one shouldn't favor too much on either gentleness or firmness alone so that he can truly appreciate the "good/bad" of them. Remember, gentleness versus firmness is not a situation, but gentleness/firmness as oneness in YIN YANG CHI (Kung Fu martial art).

attainment [ə'teɪnmənt] *n.* 达到

interplay ['ɪntəpleɪ] *n.* 相互作用

pedal ['pedl] *n.* 踏板；脚蹬子

simultaneously [ˌsɪməl'teɪnɪəsli] *adv.* 同时地；一壁；齐；一齐

release [rɪ'liːs] *v.* 释放；松开；发泄

isolate ['aɪsəleɪt] *vt.* 使隔离，使孤立；

coalescent [kəʊə'lesnt] *adj.* 接合的，结合的，合并的

Reading Comprehension.

Choose the best answer according to the text.

1. What is the relationship between *yin* and *yang*?

   A. Be opposite.

B. Mutually complementary and interdependent.

C. To interact with each other.

D. Mutual promotion.

2. What is *yin*?

   A. Firmness.　　　　　　　　B. External.

   C. Light.　　　　　　　　　　D. Internal.

3. What do the white spot on the black part and the black spot on the white one imply?

   A. The Balance.　　　　　　　B. The Extremes.

   C. The Forces.　　　　　　　 D. The Changing.

4. When the movement of *yin/yang* flows into extremes, what will happen?

   A. *Yin/yang* will start again.

   B. *Yin/yang* will change into the other side of it.

   C. The strong force will occur.

   D. The opponent will be defeated.

5. In the art of Kung Fu, the movement of *yin/yang*, such as firmness and gentleness is _____?

   A. oneness　　　　　　　　　 B. isolated

   C. opposite　　　　　　　　　D. situation

Chi (Qi)

As we understand the essence of chi, we come to appreciate what it means to build our vital life force. Chi is the energy that keeps us alive and healthy. Chi is our life force. It is derived and generated from what we eat and drink. It is a result of what we do and think. It is affected by the people and environment all around us. It is molded by the thoughts and intentions that we carry with us from moment to moment.

1. Chi is accumulated via food, water and air.
2. Chi is conserved by rest and knowledge.
3. Chi is used by action and thought.

Some people think that only living creatures have chi, but that is not so. Everything has chi, even the rocks, the water, the tree, and the animals. Some have it in extremely low amounts. Inanimate objects have chi but it is too low to give them the power to move around, eat or reproduce. People have used crystal rocks to cure sick people; they use the chi of the crystal to energize the patients.

The more chi you have, the more abilities you possess. Thus, plants have more of it than rocks, which enables them to grow and manufacture food. Animals have more of it than plants, which gives them abilities to move and make sounds. Humans have the maximum amount of chi, which enables them to think and be creative.

Chi Kung (Qi Gong)

When we speak of Chi Kung; firstly, we should understand what the essence of chi is. There are many kinds of chi, but Chinese culture emphasizes that the most basic onc is "Yuan chi (Qi)"—the origin of all living things. Yuan chi is an engine or anchor for human growth, metabolism and physical development. Yuan chi also plays an important role in defending illnesses. So, Chinese medicine teaches that the life all depends on the circulation of chi.

Chi Kung is the art of developing vital energy, particularly for health, **vitality**, mind expansion and spiritual cultivation.

There are various schools of Chi Kung, such as Shaolin Damo Chi Kung, Shaolin Cosmos Chi Kung, and Taiji Eighteen Steps Chi Kung, Flying Crane Chi Kung, and so on. Sometimes, people may refer to different Chi Kung techniques, as different types of Chi Kung, in which case there are thousands of them.

There are many wonderful benefits derived from practicing Chi Kung, and they may be generalized into the following five categories.

1. Promoting health and preventing illness.
2. Promoting longevity and youthfulness.
3. Enhancing vitality and developing internal force.
4. Expanding the mind and the **intellect**.
5. Spiritual cultivation.

Chi Kung is founded on a whole life outlook, related to the law of nature. When practicing it, you mainly have the **initiative** of your own consciousness. The content includes three adjustments.

1. Adjusting your mind to peace.

---

vitality [vaɪˈtæləti]
n. 生命力；活力；热情

intellect [ˈɪntəlekt]
n. 智力

initiative [ɪˈnɪʃətɪv]
n. 主动性；积极性；自发性

2. Adjusting your body to the best condition.

3. Adjusting your breath in balance.

If you keep training regularly and persisting, gradually the function of many parts of your body will be greatly enhanced and step by step, your health condition will be improved. The practice is able to improve quality of life and naturally **transmute** and develop a deeper awareness of subtle energies.

YIN YANG CHI (Kung Fu) Martial arts are composed of internal and external components. Internal Martial arts refer to Chi Kung. External Martial arts refer to forms, fighting with hands and weapons. When achieving a high level, you will get a wonderful combination between internal and external refinement.

Practicing Chi Kung can strengthen your body and help you against the entire force, which can help you in combat or competition.

> transmute
> [trænz'mju:t]
> v. (使)变化，变质，变形

Reading Comprehension.

Decide whether the following statements are true (T) or false (F).

1. Only living creatures have chi. _____

2. Chi is affected by the environment all around us. _____

3. The more chi you have, the less energy you have. _____

4. People can use inanimate objects to cure a certain disease. _____

5. There are many types of Chi Kung, in which case there are thousands of them. _____

6. When practicing Chi Kung, you need to adjust your body to the best condition and disobey the law of nature. _____

7. Prastising Chi Kung could develop a deeper awareness of minor

energies. _____

8. Chi Kung can keep good health for the body, but it can not give any help to the human mind. _____
9. Chi Kung is a kind of external martial art. _____
10. A very high level of Kung Fu must have a combination between internal *qi* and external force. _____

Wudang Kung Fu

Wudang Kung Fu is connected with Taoism, which emphasizes cultivating a **regimen** that helps prolong life.

Taoism is not just a school of thought, but also a philosophical, intellectual, spiritual, and folk tradition that, in different times and places, has taken on very different meanings.

As the **indigenous** Chinese religion, it can date back some 1,800 years to Master Zhang Taoling, of the Eastern Han dynasty (25–220), who organized a religious form of Taoism. Over the many years of evolution, it has had a profound influence on classical Chinese society and still functions today.

The famous Taoist works are the Lao-tzu and Chuang-tzu, which are actually academic works, but the notion of the Tao that they **preach** projects an image of the highest universal principle, a symbol of the mystery.

By continuing to exercise with Wudang Kung Fu and respect martial arts teachings, one can develop one's potential and wisdom and be more strong-minded, healthy, able to resist disease, and prolong life.

---

regimen [ˈredʒɪmən]
n. 养生法；养生之道

indigenous [ɪnˈdɪdʒənəs] *adj.*
土生土长的；生来的，固有的

preach [priːtʃ]
v. 布道，讲道；宣扬；说教；讲（道）

The Kung Fu at Wudang has the following styles: Wudang Taiji boxing, form-and-will boxing, eight-diagram palm, Wudang taiyi five-element boxing, simplified Wudang boxing, Wudang taiyi peripatetic palm, Wudang sword, Wudang taiyi whisk, Wudang xuanwu cudgel, Wudang sword of the eight drunken immortals, and the nine directions eighteen-elbow, among others.

Wudang Inner School Boxing

Wudang Inner School Boxing, which originated on Wudang Mountain, is already known in China and abroad as the mountain's natural scenery and **majestic** ancient building.

It is said that the renowned Taoist Zhang Sanfeng founded Wudang Inner School Boxing. One day, Zhang Sanfeng was **meditating** in a **thatched** hut when he suddenly heard a magpie chirping. The magpie was focusing on a snake lying on the ground. The snake raised its head and looked up at the magpie. After a while, the magpie threw itself at the snake and pecked at it. The snake dodged the attack by moving its head unflappably. As he watched this, Zhang Sanfeng wondered why the ferocious magpie could not beat the soft snake. Then he watched the magpie and found that the snake could dodge the magpie's attacks because it knew how to use quietness to defeat movement and use softness to defeat firmness, which was precisely the philosophy of Laozi *Daodejing*. Imitating the fight between the magpie and the snake and incorporating the meditation of Taoism's Mysterious Gate sect, Zhang Sanfeng created a

---

majestic
［məˈdʒestɪk］ adj.
宏伟的；壮丽的；
庄重的；磅礴

meditate ［ˈmedɪteɪt］
v. 深思，沉思，冥想

thatch ［θætʃ］ vt.
用茅草盖（房子等）的屋顶

special kind of boxing based on the theory of using quietness to defeat movement and of using softness to defeat firmness.

Since this kind of boxing originated on Wudang Mountain, it was called Wudang Boxing and, because it emphasizes inner cultivation, people also call it Wudang Inner School Boxing. Forms of Wudang Inner School Boxing practiced nowadays include the popular Taiji Quan or Shadow Boxing, Xingyi Quan or "mental form" boxing, and Wudang Sword.

Taiji Sword of Wudang Mountain

Have you ever seen the martial **prowess** of the statue of Zhenwu, the Taoist god on Wudang Mountain, who is holding a double-edged sword in his hand, standing on a stone base carved in the shape of a tortoise and a snake and looking down at man's world?

A story goes that long long ago, **demons** and ghosts ran wild for a time around the place of Wudang Mountain, causing the local people untold suffering. Hearing the news, the Jade Emperor, the Supreme Deity of Taoism, sent Ziwei, Emperor the Great, and Zhenwu, God of northern Lunar Mansions, to conquer the devils on Wudang Mountain.

Receiving a seven-star sword and instructions from the Jade Emperor, the God of Zhenwu swung his **fabulous** sword for a sweep and the jade-like **dome** was cleared of all devils wide and deep. Thereafter, the seven-star sword was named Taiji sword and handed down as an **heirloom** and one of the ritual implements of Taoism.

Nowadays, Taiji swords are widely used in martial

arts as one of the weapons. On Wudang Mountain, visitors can see several places whose names are connected with the sword, such as the Platform of Sword-Bestow, the Sword-trial Stone and the View-stand of Sword Playing.

Like Taiji boxing, Taiji swordsmanship has the advantage of "overwhelming the hard by the soft" and "attacking the moving power with static force". A master sword player can perform a sword dance so well that the sword seems invisible in the quick but gentle action. Sometimes you can hardly see the player **dazzled** by the **brandishing** sword. The outstanding series of skills and tricks in sword playing are the Snake-like Wudang Sword Art, the Sword Skill of Taiyi and Taiji Phoenix Sword Skill.

dazzle ['dæzl]
v. (强光等) 使目眩，眼花；使惊叹

brandish
['brændɪʃ] vt.
挥舞；炫耀

Reading Comprehension.

Read the text and fill in the blanks.

1. Wudang Kung Fu is connected with _____.

2. The famous Taoist academic works are _____.

3. By practicing Wudang Kung Fu, one could develop one's _____ and be more _____, healthy, able to _____ disease, and _____ life.

4. Zhang Sanfeng created a special kind of boxing based on the theory of using quietness to defeat movement and of using _____ to defeat _____.

5. Nowadays, _____ are widely used in martial arts as one of the weapons.

Part III Viewing

Why We Love Chinese Kung Fu?

Watch a short video and discuss the following questions.

- What is the meaning of the Chinese character "武"?
- What are the core Chinese values in Chinese Kung Fu?
- Why has Wushu been included in PE courses at Chinese schools and colleges?
- Why is Chinese Kung Fu popular and has won acclaim from people all over the world?
- How do you understand the sentence "We are the last people to ever pick a fight and the first people to avoid a fight"?

Part IV Further Reading

Origin and History of Chinese Kung Fu

The martial arts have a long history in China. As the Chinese name wushu suggests, martial arts are thought to have developed as methods for hand-to-hand combat used by ancient Chinese soldiers.

According to legend, martial arts were introduced in China by the Yellow Emperor during the Xia dynasty (2070 BC−1600 BC). The very first mention of Chinese martial arts occurs in the *Spring and Autumn Annals*, a court chronicle that dates all the way back to the 5th century BC.

The Spirit of Chinese Kung Fu

Endurance is the chief spirit of Chinese Kung Fu, which means the people who learn Kung Fu must try their best to avoid violence, even though their enemies may be much weaker than themselves. Chinese people always think harmony is the highest priority, which is also one of the spirits of Buddhism. The Shaolin Temple was built by Buddhist monks, so people who want to learn Kung Fu in the Shaolin Temple must accept the Buddhist spirits.

New Kung Fu students must learn endurance first by carrying water from the foot of a mountain to the top of a mountain, reciting Buddhist scriptures or even being beaten by their masters. They can never learn to fight until they can face these hardships peacefully.

The Aim of Chinese Kung Fu

The aim of Chinese Kung Fu is to avoid violence. If you can successfully persuade your enemies by words, never use Kung Fu.

A Window into Chinese culture

Due to their connections with Chinese philosophy, religion and history, Chinese martial arts provide a fascinating window into traditional Chinese culture.

One of the best ways to understand China, Chinese culture and the

Chinese martial arts is to experience them for yourself. Studying Chinese martial arts is a great way to gain a deeper understanding of Chinese culture.

Part V Practising

Translation.

Translate the following paragraphs into English or Chinese.

　　功夫（Kung Fu）是中国武术（martial arts）的俗称。中国武术的起源可以追溯到自卫的需要、狩猎活动以及古代中国的军事训练。它是中国传统体育运动的一种，年轻人和老年人都练。它已逐渐演变成了中国文化的独特元素。作为中国的国宝，武术有上百种风格，是世界上练得最多的武术形式。有些风格模仿了动物的动作，还有一些则受到了中国哲学思想、神话和传说的启发。

　　Chinese Kung Fu, a valuable cultural heritage of the Chinese nation, is a traditional sport event with unique ethnic characteristics. Taking in the essence of Confucianism and Taoism, it embodies ancient people's comprehension of life and the universe. It is not only a fighting technique, but also represents a spirit—the persistence and perseverance of Chinese people. In the 1960s, Bruce Lee blended Chinese Kung Fu with Hollywood movies, making it well known to the World. These Kung Fu movies shouldered the responsibility of spreading Chinese culture. Nowadays, lots of foreigners consider that Chinese Kung Fu is full of wonder and magic, so they have a keen interest in learning it.

Writing.

　　For this part, you are allowed to write ***a letter to a foreign friend who wants to learn Chinese Kung Fu.*** You should write at least 120 words but no more than 180 words.

Unit 9

Chinese Tea Culture

Learning Objectives

After learning this unit, you will be able to:
- learn the history and types of Chinese tea;
- learn tea manners;
- know about the Ancient Tea-horse Road and the Silk Road;
- introduce Chinese tea culture in English.

Tea-drinking is a constituent part of Chinese culture. China is an original producer of tea and is renowned for its skills in planting and making tea. Its customs of tea-drinking spread over to Europe and to many other regions through cultural exchange via the ancient Silk Road and other channels of trade. The Chinese nation has written a brilliant page for its tea culture in the history of world civilization. The development and promotion of tea has been one of China's principal contributions to the world.

Part I **Lead-in**

Watch the short video of **Tea** and choose the best choice.

1. Where was tea originated from?

   A. China.   B. Japan.

   C. Korea.   D. Britain.

2. What is the most important taste of tea?

   A. Sour.   B. Sweet.

   C. Bitter. D. Hot.

3. What is necessary for making tea? (multiple choice)

   A. Water.   B. Wares.

   C. Tea.   D. Fire.

4. What are the tea sets widely used in China? (multiple choice)
   A. Chinaware.   B. Purple clay.
   C. Glass.   D. Wood.
5. Black tea can be translated as _____.
   A. 黑茶   B. 红茶   C. 青茶   D. 普洱茶

Work in groups and discuss the following questions.

- Could you give a brief introduction to Chinese tea culture?
- What kind of tea do you like best?
- What are the seven necessities for Chinese people to begin a day?
- Do you know any poems about Chinese tea?

Part II Reading

Journey into the World of Chinese Tea

China is **synonymous** with tea, and tea with China. In fact, the history of tea in China is almost as long as the history of China itself. Despite the recent rise of coffee, Chinese tea culture continues to enjoy great popularity.

The History of Tea in China

Shennong: The Mythical Father of Chinese Medicine

The history of Chinese tea begins with Shennong, a mythical personage said to be the father of Chinese agriculture and traditional Chinese medicine.

Legend has it that Shennong **accidentally** discovered tea as he was boiling water to drink while sitting under a **camellia sinensis tree**. Some leaves from the tree fell into the water, **infusing** it with a refreshing **aroma**. Shennong

---

synonymous
[sɪˈnɒnɪməs] *adj.*
同义的，类义的；
同义词的

accidentally
[ˌæksɪˈdentəli]
adv. 偶然地，意外地，非故意地

camellia sinensis tree
山茶树；茶树

infuse [ɪnˈfjuːz] *vi.*
沏（茶），泡（草药）

aroma [əˈrəʊmə]
n. 芳香，香味；气派，风格

took a sip, found it enjoyable, and thus, tea was born. Shennong is considered the father of Chinese agriculture.

Early Archeological and Historical Evidence

Chinese mythology aside, **archeological** evidence has been found indicating that tea was used as a medicine by the **elite** as early as the Han dynasty (206 BC–220 AD).

Tea didn't achieve widespread popularity as an everyday **beverage** in China until the Tang dynasty (618–907), however. Chinese Buddhist monks were some of the first to develop the habit of drinking tea. Its caffeine content helped them concentrate during long hours of prayer and **meditation**.

The Classic of Tea by Lu Yu

Much of the information we have about early Chinese tea culture comes from *The Classic of Tea*（《茶经》）, written around 760 by Lu Yu（陆羽）, an orphan who grew up cultivating and drinking tea in a Buddhist **monastery**.

The Classic of Tea describes early Tang dynasty tea culture and explains how to grow and prepare tea.

In Lu Yu's day, tea leaves were compressed into tea bricks, which were sometimes used as **currency**. When it was time to drink the tea, it was ground into a powder and mixed with water using a **whisk** to create a **frothy** beverage.

Although this type of powdered tea is no longer common in China, it was brought from China to Japan during the Tang dynasty and lives on today in Japanese **matcha**.

Tea During the Ming and Qing Dynasties

During the Ming dynasty (1368−1644), tea bricks were replaced with loose by imperial **decree**. This change was meant to make life easier for farmers since the traditional method of creating tea bricks was quite labor **intensive**.

Loose leaf tea is still the most common form of tea found in China today.

Tea was introduced in Britain in the mid-1600s and British demand for tea soon created a trade imbalance with China. To correct it, Britain began exporting **opium** to China.

After China tried to ban opium, Britain launched the mid-19th century Opium Wars to force the trade to continue.

---

monastery [ˈmɒnəstri] n. 修道院，寺院

currency [ˈkʌrənsi] n. 货币；通用，流通，传播

whisk [wɪsk] n. 搅拌器

frothy [ˈfrɒθi] adj. 起泡的，多泡的，空洞的

matcha [ˈmætʃə] n. 日本抹茶；抹茶

decree [dɪˈkriː] n. 法令，命令

intensive [ɪnˈtensɪv] adj. 加强的，强烈的

opium [ˈəʊpiəm] n. 鸦片；麻醉剂

The East India Company and Robert Fortune

Although the wars achieved their stated goal, British merchants began to worry about the **viability** of continuing to rely on tea from the Chinese market. Soon, the East India Company sent Robert Fortune, a Scottish botanist and adventurer, to steal the secrets of tea-making from China.

Fortune's stolen information, plants and seeds were then used to start large-scale tea production in India.

Indian tea production quickly **outstripped** that of China, and China lost its long-standing **monopoly** on the international tea trade.

The Chinese tea industry went into decline, and China has only recently regained its status as the world's leading tea exporter.

Popular Types of Tea in China

Today, most Chinese tea is loose leaf tea that's **steeped** in boiling water, either in a teapot or directly in a thermos or glass, depending on the type of tea being consumed. Drinking tea made from tea bags is uncommon in China.

Tea is used as a catch-all term for many different herbal brews in the West. In the strictest sense, however, the word "tea" only applies to beverages made from the leaves of the Camellia sinensis plant.

Contrary to popular belief, the differences in taste and color seen in different types of Chinese tea are not due to the use of different kinds of tea leaves. Rather, they are due to differences in the production and manufacturing process.

Types of Chinese teas

The type of tea produced is determined by the level of **oxidation** the tea leaves are allowed to undergo before the process is stopped by heating the leaves. In China, tea merchants usually refer to this oxidation process as fermentation.

oxidation [ˌɒksɪˈdeɪʃn] n. 氧化

Chinese teas are classified according to their level of fermentation. The more fermented the tea, the stronger its taste. White teas are essentially unfermented. They are followed by lightly fermented green teas, half fermented oolong teas and fully fermented black teas.

Pu'er (also called pu-erh) teas, which are generally quite dark and strong, are said to be post-fermented.

Certain regions of China are known for producing and consuming special types of tea. For example, Wuyi Mountain, in Fujian Province, is particularly famous for production and consumption of fine oolong teas, such as Dahongpao.

Green teas such as Biluochun, grown in Jiangsu Province, are popular in the region around Shanghai.

We must not forget herbal "teas". Other beverages referred to as "tea" also exist in China, although some of them don't actually contain any camellia sinensis leaves. Barley tea, made from roasted barley grains, doesn't actually contain any tea leaves at all.

Other types of "tea" that enjoy immense popularity among the younger generations are milk tea and bubble tea. These sugary drinks, which don't contain much (if any) actual tea, come in a variety of different flavors.

Modern Chinese Tea Culture

Tea culture in China is most **intact** in the south, where the bulk of China's tea is produced. Tea can be consumed at home or in teahouses, many of which offer private rooms for drinking tea with friends or business partners. Although tea is consumed by people from every sector of society, most tea connoisseurs tend to be middle-aged business people, **intellectuals** or artists.

Chinese Tea Ceremonies Gain in Popularity

Much of modern Chinese tea culture revolves around the gongfu tea ceremony. Thought to have originated in Fujian or Guangdong Province, it usually features black, oolong or pu'er tea. At its most basic, the ceremony makes use of tiny tea cups, a tea-brewing vessel such as a gaiwan or an Yixing purple clay teapot, a tea strainer, a tea pitcher and a tea table or tray. Other utensils such as tea tongs are optional.

The more complicated the ceremony, the more utensils are likely to be involved. Tea tables are often quite large and can be decorated with whimsical tea pets.

How to Conduct a Chinese Tea Ceremony

Normally, tea ceremonies are run by a host who begins by steeping loose leaf tea in water in a gaiwan or teapot, and then pouring it through a tea strainer into a tea pitcher to filter out bits of tea leaf.

Next, the host pours tea from the pitcher onto teacups. Instead of serving this first batch of tea to guests, the host generally pours it out onto the tea table, allowing it to drain into a bucket underneath.

---

intact [ɪnˈtækt]
adj. 完整无缺的，未经触动的，未受损伤的

intellectual [ˌɪntəˈlektʃuəl] *n.* 知识分子；脑力劳动者；有极高智力的人

> discard [dɪsˈkɑːd]
> vt. 丢弃，抛弃；解雇；出牌

This is done to wash the tea cups and also because tea from the first pour is thought to be too strong to drink. This process is then repeated, except that the tea is served to those present instead of being **discarded**.

After being served, guests should either thank the host verbally or express thanks by tapping their bent index and middle fingers on the tea table. This custom is most common in southern China and is said to have originated during the Qing dynasty (1644—1911), when the Qianlong Emperor, who was traveling in disguise, poured tea for a servant.

The servant wanted to show his gratitude by kneeling, but couldn't do so for fear of revealing the emperor's identity. Therefore, he tapped the table with two bent fingers instead.

> entrench [ɪnˈtrentʃ]
> v. 用壕沟围绕或保护……；牢固地确立……

For now, tea drinking is firmly **entrenched** in Chinese culture.

Reading Comprehension.

Decide whether the following statements are true (T) or false (F).

1. It is said that Shennong was the father of Traditional Chinese Medicine. _____
2. Tea has been popularly drunk in China since the Han dynasty. _____
3. During the Tang dynasty, Chinese tea was compressed into bricks and brought to Japan and lives on today in Japanese matcha. _____
4. Britain launched the mid-19th century Opium Wars to deal with the trade imbalance. _____
5. Large-scale tea production in India made the Chinese tea industry lose its world's leading status in the 19th century. _____
6. The more fermented the tea, the stronger its taste. _____

7. Oolong tea is unfermented type of tea. _____

8. Dahongpao is a fine oolong tea in Jiangsu Province. _____

Work in groups and discuss the following questions.

> - Could you tell the story of Shen Nong?
> - Could you tell the origin of Dahongpao?
> - How to make a pot of gongfu tea?
> - Why do the guests tap their bent fingers on the table?
> - Which is popular beverage among young Chinese people? Whether coffee poses a great threat to Chinese tea culture?

Chinese Tea Making Joins UNESCO List

The tea that has delighted and fascinated the world for millennia has finally received top-level global recognition as a shared cultural treasure of mankind.

Traditional tea processing techniques and their associated social practices in China were added to UNESCO's Representative List of the Intangible Cultural Heritage of Humanity. The status was conferred by the Intergovernmental Committee for the Safeguarding of Intangible Cultural Heritage, hosted in Rabat, Morocco. It consists of knowledge, skills and practices concerning management of tea plantations, the picking of tea leaves, and the processing, drinking and sharing of tea.

According to UNESCO, in China traditional tea processing techniques are closely associated with geographical location and natural environment, resulting in a distribution range between 18° N−37° N and 94° E−122° E. The techniques are mainly found in the provinces and autonomous regions of Zhejiang, Jiangsu, Jiangxi, Hunan, Anhui, Hubei, Henan, Shaanxi, Yunnan,

Guizhou, Sichuan, Fujian, Guangdong and Guangxi. Associated social practices, however, are spread throughout the country and shared by multiple ethnic groups.

Over 2,000 tea varieties, mainly in six categories—green, black, yellow, oolong, white and dark—are grown in China. Core skills include shaqing (enzyme inactivation), menhuang (yellowing), wodui (pealing), weidiao (withering), zuoqing (leaves shaking and cooling), fajiao (oxidation or fermentation) and yinzhi (scenting). Tea-related customs are not only found across the country, but also influenced the rest of the world through the ancient Silk Road and trade routes. As a document from the Ministry of Culture and Tourism to UNESCO explained, tea is ubiquitous in Chinese people's daily life. Steeped or boiled tea is served in homes, workplaces, tea houses, restaurants, temples and used as an important medium for communication in socializing and ceremonies such as weddings, apprentice-taking and sacrifices. "Practices of greeting guests with tea and building good relationships within families and among neighborhoods through tea-related activities are shared among multiple ethnic groups, and provide a sense of identity and continuity for communities, groups and individuals concerned," the document said.

In China, 44 registered national-level intangible cultural heritage entries are related to tea. There are over 40 vocational colleges and 80 universities in China that have set up majors in tea science or tea culture, resulting in over 3,000 graduates specializing in tea production and art every year, according to the ministry.

The inscription of the element is the 43rd entry from China on the Representative List of the Intangible Cultural Heritage of Humanity, whose total tops all other countries.

Part III Listening and Speaking

Listen to the conversation and choose the best answer to each of the questions.

1. Where did Jason learn the riddle of tea leaves?

    A. At a tea ceremony.

    B. From a book about tea.

    C. In his Chinese culture class.

    D. From his conversation with Li Ping.

2. How long have people in China been drinking tea?

    A. For hundreds of years.

    B. For thousands of years.

    C. Since the Ming dynasty.

    D. Since the Qing dynasty.

3. What are Jason and Li Ping mainly talking about?

    A. The ceremony of tea in China.

    B. The birthplace of tea in China.

    C. The popularity of tea in China.

    D. The development of tea in China.

Work in groups and answer the following questions in English.

- What is the riddle in the conversation?
- Could you introduce the Chinese tea culture briefly?

Listen to the passage and fill in the blanks with the exact words you hear.

China is the earliest country in the world to have planted tea and the (1) _____ homeland of tea culture. Thanks to different geographic (2) _____, Chinese people have developed different varieties of tea with (3) _____ flavors.

How do Chinese people prepare and serve tea? Gongfu Cha means "making tea with skill". It is a popular method of preparing and (4) _____ tea in China. It makes use of small Yixing teapots to prepare and serve the (5) _____. (6) _____, water quality and (7) _____ are the two most important (8) _____ that have to be considered while brewing tea. The (9) _____ is mostly applicable to Oolong teas. The custom of tea-drinking spread from China to other countries through cultural exchanges via the (10) _____ Tea-horse Road and other trade channels.

Part IV Viewing

New Words		
tread	[tred]	v. 踩成；踏出；步行于；踩（烂）
plateau	[ˈplætəu]	n. 高原；平稳时期，稳定水平；停滞期
tranquility	[trænˈkwɪlɪtɪ]	n. 平静；安静；安宁；平稳
canyon	[ˈkænjən]	n. 峡谷
static	[ˈstætɪk]	adj. 静止的；不变的；静电的
migration	[maɪˈgreɪʃn]	n. 迁移，移居
desolation	[ˌdesəˈleɪʃn]	n. 遗弃，荒凉；破坏；凄凉
exquisite	[ɪkˈskwɪzɪt]	adj. 精致的；剧烈的；敏锐的
hoof	[hu:f]	n.（兽的）蹄，马蹄
imposing	[ɪmˈpəuzɪŋ]	adj. 印象深刻的；壮观的，威风的
indiscernible	[ˌɪndɪˈsɜ:nəbl]	adj. 难辨认的，觉察不出的

Watch a short video of the **Ancient Tea-horse Road** and choose the best choice.

1. Commodities except _____ flowed to the outside world through the Ancient Tea-horse Road.
   A. tea   B. furs
   C. mask   D. horses and cows

2. the Ancient Tea-horse Road first appeared during the _____ dynasty.
   A. Song   B. Yuan
   C. Ming and Qing D. Tang

3. From ancient times, _____ have been the main vehicles used for transportation year after year.
   A. mabang caravans B. horses
   C. automobiles   D. cows

4. The Ancient Tea-horse Road features _____.
   A. many moutains   B. the scenery
   C. peculiar stones D. marvelous clouds

5. The accomplishment of _____ make the Ancient Tea-horse Road become a part of history, but the cultural and historic values still remain.

A. the Qinghai-Tibet Highway and the Yunnan-Lhasa Highway

B. the Sichun-Lhasa Highway and the Chengdu-Lhasa Highway

C. the Yunnan-Tibet Highway and the Chengdu-Lhasa Highway

D. the Sichun-Tibet Highway and the Yunnan-Lhasa Highway

Part V Practising

Translation.

Translate the following paragraphs into Chinese.

茶拥有5000年的历史。传说，神农氏喝开水时，几片野叶子落进壶里，开水顿时散发出宜人的香味。他喝了几口，觉得很提神。茶就这样被发现了。自此，茶在中国开始流行。茶园遍布全国，茶商变得富有。昂贵、雅致的茶具成了地位的象征。今天，茶不仅是一种健康的饮品，而且是中国文化的一个组成部分。越来越多的国际游客一边品茶，一边了解中国文化。

Shennong, a legendary hero, tasted hundreds of wild plants to see which were poisonous and which were edible, so as to prevent people from eating the poisonous plants. It is said that he was poisoned seventy-two times in one day but was saved by chewing some tender leaves of an evergreen plant blossoming with white flowers. Since he had a transparent belly, people could see how the food moved throughout his stomach and intestines. When they saw the juice of the tender leaves go up and down in the stomach as if it were searching for something, they called it "cha", meaning search in Chinese. Later it was renamed "cha" having the same sound of the present one.

Writing.

Suppose you are Li Hua. Your American friend Jack sent you an email to learn about the common sense of Chinese tea culture. Now, please send him an email, which includes:

1. Introduction to Chinese Tea culture;
2. The benefits of drinking tea;
3. Invite him to experience the tea culture in China.

Unit 10

Chinese Cuisine

Learning Objectives

After learning this unit, you will be able to:
- learn the basic theory of *yin* and *yang* in Chinese food;
- try to introduce China's Eight Great Cuisines in English;
- try to know the features and typical dishes of China's Eight Great Cuisines.

Chinese cuisine is an important part of Chinese culture, which includes cuisines originating from the diverse regions of China, as well as from Chinese people in other parts of the world. The most praised Four Major Cuisines are Chuan, Lu, Yue and Huaiyang, representing West, North, South and East China cuisine correspondingly. Modern Eight Great Cuisines of China are Anhui, Cantonese, Fujian, Hunan, Jiangsu, Shandong, Sichuan, and Zhejiang cuisines.

Color, aroma and taste are the three traditional aspects used to describe Chinese food, as well as the meaning, appearance and nutrition of the food. Cooking should be appraised from ingredients used, cuttings, cooking time and seasoning.

It is considered inappropriate to use knives on the dining table in China. Chopsticks are the main eating utensils for Chinese food, which can be used to cut and pick up food.

Part I Lead-in

*Watch a short video of **A Bite of China** and discuss the following questions.*

- Do you like the CCTV programme *A Bite of China*? Why?
- Can you tell the differences between northern and southern parts of Chinese food?
- Can you tell the differences between Chinese and western food?

Match the following cooking methods with the Chinese meaning.

1. 煮　_____　A. roasting and barbecuing

2. 炖，煨，焖　_____　B. steaming

3. 烘　_____　C. stir-frying

4. 蒸　_____　D. frying

5. 扒　_____　E. stewing

6. 煎　_____　F. deep-frying

7. 炒　_____　G. boiling

8. 烤　_____　H. baking

9. 炸　_____　I. frying and simmering

10. 熏　_____　J. smoking

Part II Reading

The *Yin & Yang* of Chinese Cuisine

accentuate
[əkˈsentʃueɪt] *vt.*
强调，着重指出

condiment
[ˈkɒndɪmənt] *n.*
调味品，佐料

Besides **accentuating** the natural flavors of ingredients through sauces, **condiments** and cooking techniques, Chinese cuisine also emphasizes the harmony of cooling and warming foods to provide the right balance of nutrition and energy that ensures general wellness. Every meal should satisfy your taste buds, fill your belly, and help maintain good health for the whole family.

ingrain [ˈɪnˈgreɪn]
vt. 使根深蒂固

This philosophy is derived from Taoism, and has been deeply **ingrained** in Chinese culture for thousands of years; and has also influenced Korean and Vietnamese cuisines as well. It is the belief that all things contain *yin* and *yang* energies and through the **congruence** of this duality, we may achieve true harmony in our lives, as well as ensure the well-being of our bodies.

You've probably seen the round black & white symbol before. *Yin* is associated with the feminine, softness, and cooling energy, represented by the black half. Whereas the white half symbolizes the masculine, warmth, and strength. Neither is actually positive nor negative but embodies the dual aspects of the universe. Nothing is purely *yin* nor *yang*, just that some are primary one more than the other.

Yin or cooling foods tend to be bitter, sour or salty, contain more moisture, and come in cool-toned colors such as green and purple. Fish, cucumber, leafy greens, lemongrass, tofu, lotus and soy sauce are some examples.

Yang or warming foods are dry, sweet, spicy or **pungent**, usually grown closer to the soil, and in warm-toned colors like red, yellow, brown and orange. Examples include meat, potatoes, **papaya**, chilies, **galangal** and ginger.

Cooking methods have *yin* and *yang* properties as well: stir-fry, deep-fry, roasting and **grilling** are considered *yang* while steaming and boiling are *yin*.

With all that in mind, you can probably guess that Chinese food habits also correspond to the seasons—*yin* foods to cool off in the hot summer, and *yang* foods to warm up in the winter. When you're down with the common cold, it is best to consume more warming *yang* foods to balance the excess of *yin* energy in your body. Too much heat can

---

congruence ['kɒŋgruəns] *n.* 适合；一致

pungent ['pʌndʒənt] *adj.* 辛辣的；刺激性的

papaya [pə'paɪə] *n.* 番木瓜树，番木瓜果

galangal [gə'læŋgəl] *n.* 高良姜，山奈

grill ['grɪl] *v.* 烧烤

Vocabulary	
pimple ['pɪmpl] n. 丘疹，粉刺，小脓疱	
alleviate [ə'liːvieɪt] v. 减轻；缓解	
veggies ['vegɪz] abbr. vegetables 蔬菜	
broths [brɔːθs] n. 肉汤	
garnish ['gɑːnɪʃ] vt. 装饰，文饰；给……加配菜	

cause dry lips and **pimples**, and eating more cooling *yin* foods can help **alleviate** such conditions.

As mentioned, authentic Chinese dishes incorporate both *yin* and *yang* ingredients to achieve the balance of various flavors. Meat dishes are always accompanied with **veggies**; soups and **broths** are usually **garnished** with spring onions or scallions, and spicy delicacies are often complemented with cooling greens. Also, like most Asians, Chinese people love to dine together with their families—a table full of multiple dishes that include rice or noodles, vegetables, meat or fish, and a steamy, hearty bowl of soup or broth for everyone to savor.

So, plan your next meal with the philosophy of *yin* and *yang* for more wholesome, hearty enjoyment.

Reading Comprehension.

Decide whether the following statements are true (T) or false (F).

1. Chinese cuisine emphasizes the harmony of *yin* and *yang* foods to maintain people's health. _____
2. This philosophy of *yin* & *yang* is derived from Confucianism and has been deeply ingrained in Chinese culture for thousands of years. _____
3. Different cooking methods also influence the balance of the Chinese diet. _____
4. Tofu is one of the *yang* foods. _____
5. It is better to consume more cooling *yin* foods in the winter. _____
6. Full of multiple dishes of Chinese people is the reflection of prosperity and luxury. _____

Chinese Food

Chinese food is widely known for its variety and abundance with about 8,000 renowned ancient and modern dishes, 600 types of ingredients, and over 48 basic ways of cooking.

Features of Chinese Food and Cuisine

Chinese people attach particular importance to a triple principle of their food, namely, color, aroma, and taste. Color refers not only to the **hue** of a dish but also it is modeling. Food is often decorated by carving in a specific appearance, which actually requires more than a few years of hard training by chefs. Aroma involves the appetizing smell of the dishes making one's mouth water. Taste refers to utilizing suitable condiments and perfect food matches to create a unique flavor.

To achieve this standard, every **exquisite** culinary dish involves a long and complicated process from selecting the

hue [hjuː] n. 色彩，色调；外表，样子

exquisite [ɪkˈskwɪzɪt] adj. 精致的

acrobatic
[ˌækrəˈbætɪk]
adj. 杂技的

ingredients to finally serving it to diners. The superb skills of Chinese chefs make a great contribution to the development of the Chinese food industry. Sometimes, watching their work is like enjoying a splendid **acrobatic** show.

China's Regional Cooking Styles

China is vast with complex geographical features. Thus it has various regional cuisine. The most famous cooking styles in China are the Eight Great Cuisines, but there is more than that.

China's Eight Great Cuisines

From the Ming (1368–1644) to the Qing (1616–1911) dynasties, there emerged eight great cuisines respectively, from Sichuan, Hunan, Guangdong, Anhui, Fujian, Jiangsu, Shandong, and Zhejiang Provinces.

Every cuisine is distinct from others and the differences in their formation have much to do with the geography, climate, natural resources, and eating habits of the specific area.

Video linked—The Eight Great Cuisines of China

1. Sichuan Cuisine—Spicy and Numbing

Recommended Sichuan Food	Corresponding Chinese Name	Sichuan Cuisine Characteristics
Sichuan Hotpot	四川火锅	prickly ash (the numbing spice), spicy
Water Boiled Beef	水煮牛肉	
Fuqi Feipian	夫妻肺片	

　　Apart from favoring a spicy-sour, pungent flavor, Sichuan Cuisine distinguishes it from similar Hunan or Guizhou Cuisine by applying Chinese **prickly ash** seeds, leaving a special feeling of **numbness** in one's mouth.

　　And thanks to various ways of cooking, such as stir-frying and steaming, the cuisine has numerous dishes with different flavors but utilizing the same ingredients.

prickly ash
[ˈprɪkliːæʃ] 花椒
numbness
[ˈnʌmnəs] *n.*
麻木；麻痹

2. Hunan Cuisine—Spicy and Sour

Hunan Province provides a menu rich with a **potent** punch of chili, so the **uninitiated** may easily mix up the cooking styles of Hunan and Sichuan.

Recommended Hunan Food	Corresponding Chinese Name	Hunan Cuisine Characteristics
Tasty Crawfish	口味虾	pickled chilies and vegetables, sour relish
Steamed Fish Head with Diced Red Peppers	剁椒鱼头	
Steamed Ham	腊味合蒸	

Yet the special characteristics of Hunan Cuisine focus on pickled chilies and vegetables, sour **relish**, and heavier use of a kind of fatty preserved meat called larou in Chinese, tasting a bit like smoky bacon.

3. Cantonese Cuisine—Light and Refreshing

The Cantonese are widely recognized as **gourmets** as their food catalog is very extensive and varied. Because of the location of Guangdong province and its climate features, the Cantonese are fascinated by light, refreshing and **aquatic** food, in which the tender and original taste of the ingredients is kept intact.

Besides, this cuisine abounds in vegetables, and its **congee** and **dim sum** receive a warm welcome from both the public and **gastronomists**.

Recommended Cantonese Food	Corresponding Chinese Name	Cantonese Cuisine Characteristics
White Cut Chicken	白切鸡	seafood, light and refreshing taste, dim sums
Char Siu	叉烧	
Boiled Prawns	白灼虾	

gourmet [ˈguəmeɪ]
n. 美食家，讲究吃喝的人

aquatic [əˈkwætɪk]
adj. 水生的；水产的

congee [ˈkɒndʒiː]
n. 粥

dim sum [ˌdɪmˈsʌm]
点心

gastronomist
[gæsˈtrɒnəmɪst]
n. 美食家

4. Anhui Cuisine—Fresh Local Produce

The excellent geographical advantage of the Huangshan Mountains endows local people with a great deal of fresh **flora** and tasty **fauna**, composing the major ingredients of the dishes.

Anhui Cuisine chefs focus a lot of attention on preserving most of the original taste and nutrition of the materials, but they sometimes add ham or sugar candy to improve their dishes' taste.

Recommended Anhui Food	Corresponding Chinese Name	Anhui Cuisine Characteristics
Ham and Whippy Bamboo Stew	火腿炖鞭笋	abundant flora and fauna, like to add ham or sugar candy
Stewed Loach with Ham	火腿炖泥鳅	

flora ['flɔːrə] *n.* 植物群

fauna ['fɔːnə] *n.* 动物群

5. Fujian Cuisine—Often with Soup

Fujian Cuisine is sourced from the native cooking style of Fujian Province and shares a few common characteristics with nearby Taiwan and Guangdong. There's a wealth of seafood and woodland-based ingredients forming dazzling choices for diners.

The unique practice of adding red rice wine and shrimp oil to seafood, chicken, and bamboo dishes, aims at improving their flavors. Almost every dish is served with soup, just as the local saying goes: no meal is truly complete without soup（无汤不行）.

Recommended Fujian Food	Corresponding Chinese Name	Fujian Cuisine Characteristics
Stewed Chicken with Three Cups Sauce	三杯鸡	seafood, woodland-based ingredients, soup
Fo Tiao Qiang	佛跳墙	
Tai Chi Prawns	太极明虾	

6. Jiangsu Cuisine—Freshwater Seafood

Jiangsu Cuisine is a combination of both the Southern and the Northern relishes in China and the local chefs are **dexterous** in cooking both different styles of dishes.

The Yangtze River, winding throughout the region, offers plenty of produce in every season. Another characteristic of Jiangsu Cuisine is its exquisite refreshments and snacks, which cater to the taste buds of lovers of food.

In addition, Nanjing, Suzhou, and Yangzhou have been famous since ancient times. Ancient private gardens and water towns such as Zhouzhuang and Tongli are also the charms of Jiangsu Province.

Recommended Jiangsu Food	Corresponding Chinese Name	Jiangsu Cuisine Characteristics
Watermelon Chicken	西瓜鸡	freshwater seafood, plenty of river produce
Brine-Boiled Duck	盐水鸭	
Sweet and Sour Mandarin Fish	松鼠桂鱼	

dexterous
['dekstrəs] adj.
(身手)灵巧的,
敏捷的

7. Shandong Cuisine—High-Calorie and High-Protein

Shandong Cuisine, with a long history, has a great impact on other cuisines. With historical roots originating in sophisticated cuisine, the ingredients selected are more costly than those of others, usually seafood, due to the favorable location.

Besides, its long **duration** of cold weather makes local chefs skilled in producing high-calorie and high-protein dishes. Major cooking techniques are quick-fry and deep-fry, which create the distinctive crispy texture of the dishes.

duration [djuˈreɪʃn]
n. 持续时间；期间

Recommended Shandong Food	Corresponding Chinese Name	Shandong Cuisine Characteristics
Stewed Pork Hock	水晶肘子	seafood, high-calorie, and high-protein
Four Joys Meatballs	四喜丸子	

8. Zhejiang Cuisine—Mellow and Non-Greasy

Characterized by the mellow and non-greasy flavor, Zhejiang Cuisine serves as a representative of the food from along the lower Yangtze River.

Situated in the so-called "land of fish and rice", Zhejiang has a substantial scope of local produce, nutrients, and tastes for its diners. The main methods of cooking are quick frying, stir-frying, braising, and deep-frying.

Recommended Zhejiang Food	Corresponding Chinese Name	Zhejiang Cuisine Characteristics
Dongpo Pork	东坡肉	mellow and non-greasy flavor, plenty of lake produce
Shrimp Meat with Longjing Tea	龙井虾仁	
Fish Cooked in Vinegar Gravy	西湖醋鱼	
"Beggars" Chicken	叫花鸡	

Reading Comprehension.

Choose the best answer according to the text.

1. Dongpo Pork is the typical course of _____ .

    A. Anhui Cuisine   B. Shandong Cuisine

    C. Zhejiang Cuisine   D. Jiangsu Cuisine

2. Man-Han Full Banquet belongs to _____ .

    A. Zhe Cuisine   B. Lu Cuisine

    C. Xiang Cuisine   D. Su Cuisine

3. Fo Tiao Qiang is the famous dish of _____ .

    A. Hui Cuisine   B. Lu Cuisine

    C. Xiang Cuisine   D. Min Cuisine

4. The typical dish of _____ cuisine is steamed fish head with diced red peppers.

    A. Anhui Cuisine   B. Hunan Cuisine

    C. Zhejiang Cuisine   D. Sichuan Cuisine

5. The typical feature of Cantonese cuisine is _____ .

    A. spicy and numbing

    B. high-calorie and high-protein

    C. often with soup

    D. light and refreshing

6. _____ situated in the so-called "land of fish and rice".

    A. Hunan   B. Anhui

    C. Zhejiang   D. Sichuan

7. _____ Cuisine mixes both the Southern and the Northern tastes in China.

    A. Jiangsu   B. Hunan

    C. Zhejiang   D. Shandong

8. There are various regional cuisines because of _____ .

    A. geography and temperature

    B. cooking methods and materials

C. ingredients and cooking time

D. locations and climates

9. From _____ dynasty, there emerged eight great cuisines respectively.

    A. Song   B. Tang

    C. Yuan   D. Ming

10. "No meal is truly complete without soup" refers to _____ Cuisine.

    A. Guangdong   B. Zhejiang

    C. Sichuan   D. Fujian

Part III Further Reading

Chinese Dining Etiquette

As a state of ceremonies, China has always attached great importance to etiquette. Chinese dining etiquette is an important portion of Chinese food culture. Good dining etiquette and table manners can show one's good self-cultivation and leave a good impression on Chinese host. When in Rome, do as the Romans do.

Etiquette in Using Chopsticks

Chopsticks are said to be a great invention by the Chinese and nearly 30% of the world's population make use of chopsticks. They are the flexible extension of your hands, keeping your fingers clean with no grease and safe without touching extreme heat and coldness.

It is documented that properly handling chopsticks requires the coordination of over 80 joints and 50 muscles, which makes people more dexterous and intelligent.

The use of chopsticks is a must in Chinese cuisine, accompanied by some always taboos that you must have at least basic ideas:

★ Chopsticks should not be inserted into the rice and should be placed flat on the bowl owing to the Chinese practice of leaving such dishes for the dead.

★ Don't play with your chopsticks, such as using the chopsticks to beating your bowls or waving your chopsticks around in the air.

★ Don't use your chopsticks to flip the food. If you need to do so, try to use a shovel.

★ Pointing at people with your chopsticks is considered to be very impolite. Try to avoid so. If you accidentally do so, you must apologize in time.

★ Try to hold your chopsticks and avoid them falling to the ground.

★ Pick up the bowl of rice and lift the rice into your mouth with the chopsticks. Do not make any noise when chewing the food.

★ The spoon should not be used at the same time with the chopsticks.

★ Do not "dig" or "search" through one's food for something in particular. This is sometimes known as "digging one's grave" and is extremely poor manners.

★ Do not lick the food attached to the chopsticks and don't use them to move the bowl or plate.

★ Do not spear food with chopsticks.

Chinese Culinary Customs

In the West, people have taken what they like on a separate plate. Different from Westerners, Chinese people prefer to share food. The elders select food for the young; the hosts apportion the best part of the dishes to their distinguished guests to show their respect and warm welcome.

Such Chinese culinary customs add to the hospitable character of the

Chinese people. Through sharing food with guests, friends, and families, Chinese people tend to be more sensitive about the need of others at the table and often firstly take the group's needs into consideration.

Faced with the spread of the corona virus, the government is promoting using serving utensils. The authorities across the country are running advertisements with slogans like: "The distance between you and civilized dining is just one pair of serving chopsticks."

Sharing food with family and friends is just as deeply ingrained, and serving chopsticks is not seen as undermining that expression of closeness but an important manner we should observe nowadays.

Seating Arrangement

In China, people share dishes communally. In order to permit easy sharing, square and rectangular tables are normally used for small groups of people, while round tables are for large groups. If the round table is very large, then it usually has a Lazy Susan turntable to facilitate passing or serving dishes.

In a formal dinner, the seating order is very strict. Chinese seating order is based on seniority and organizational hierarchy. In general, the seat of honor is usually the one in the center facing east or facing the entrance. This seat is usually reserved for the guest with the highest status. Others with higher status sit in close proximity to the seat of honor, and those with positions sit further away. While as a host, he may take the least prominent seat, usually the one nearest the kitchen entrance or service door. Only

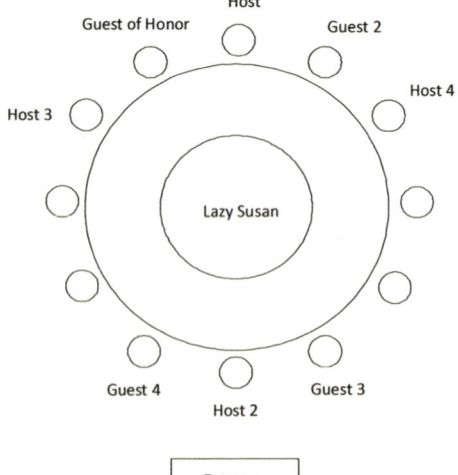

after the senior or the guest of honor sit down, other people can be seated.

How to Order Dishes Properly

If time permits, the menu can be circulated among the people in attendance and the host will make the final decision. But whether the dishes are ordered by the host or the guests, here are some basic rules that require attention.

Ask everyone's opinions: vegetarians, religious taboos, food allergies, or favorite food. Prioritize the local specialty dishes such as Roast Duck in Beijing, Braised Meatballs in Shanghai, Dim Sum in Guangdong. Balance the portion of meat dishes and vegetable dishes and try to avoid ordering food that needs to be handled by hand.

Eating Etiquette in China

Chinese people like sharing food together and all the dishes are usually placed in the center of a round table with a Lazy Susan, rather than a rectangular table like in the West. A Lazy Susan is a round rotating disc in the center of the dining table, that ensures all the diners have equal accessibility to the served meal and to makes everybody feel respected.

Here is a complete guide on eating etiquette in China:

★ Don't start eating until the host gives a sign to start.

★ When the dishes are served, you need to wait for the elders, leaders, and guests to try the dishes first.

★ Try to choose dishes that are close to you, and don't flip the dishes back and forth. If someone else is serving the food, don't put your hand over that person's hand to pick up the food.

★ You should not rotate the Lazy Susan for yourself when someone else on the table is serving himself from the main bowl. It is recommended to wait until he gets a sufficient quantity of the dish.

★ Wait until the dish takes a complete round when you want to have something a second time so that everyone gets his due share.

★ Never fill your plate to the maximum, and always serve yourself with a small quantity. Rotating the Lazy Susan counterclockwise is yet another bad habit that should be avoided.

★ Despite the facility of the Lazy Susan, it is expected of the host to offer the special dish to all the members present before he takes a share for himself, using a pair of serving chopsticks, of course, which is a simple gesture of showing concern and respect for others. Guests can politely decline or leave the food on the plate if they don't want to eat something.

★ Concentrate on the meal and the people in attendance. It is considered ill-mannered to fiddle with your phone during dining.

★ When you pick your teeth, use your hand or napkin to cover in front of your mouth.

★ Quiet and slow chewing will suggest your good manner. Talking to other people with a full mouth is also impolite.

Chinese Drinking Etiquette

In China, at the beginning of a banquet or a formal dinner, the host must first toast to the guests to show his hospitality. Wine, beer, or even soda can be used to toast.

If you wish to take a drink of wine at a formal dinner, you must first toast another dinner guest regardless of whether he or she responds by drinking. If you are toasted and don't want to drink, simply touch your lips to the edge of the wine glass to acknowledge the courtesy.

Normally, your glass will be refilled immediately following a toast in preparation for the next one.

Etiquette for Serving Tea

Tea always plays an important role at a Chinese dinner. It is usually served by a waiter or waitress as soon as you have a seat in a restaurant.

Whenever tea is served, you should say "thank you" or make a gesture of thanks—tap the table with your first two fingers twice. The host should naturally refill the empty teacups and never point the mouth of the teapot to others.

Leaving the Table

Chinese banquets commonly last for about two hours, but the dinner is over when the host stands up and offers the final toast. Then you should immediately leave after expressing your thanks to the host for his hospitality. In some cases, you can invite the host to your own future banquet.

If you want to leave in the middle of the banquet, explain the reason to your host and appreciate his hospitality. Remember: do not invite other guests to leave with you. Otherwise, the banquet will be over in advance.

New Words		
grease	[gri:s]	n. 动物油脂
dexterous	[ˈdekstrəs]	adj.（身手）灵巧的，敏捷的
taboo	[təˈbu:]	n. 禁忌；忌讳
shovel	[ˈʃʌvl]	n. 铲子，铁锹

New Words		
attach	[əˈtætʃ]	v. 贴上，系
spear	[spɪə(r)]	vt. 刺，戳
apportion	[əˈpɔːʃn]	vt. 分摊，分配
undermine	[ˌʌndəˈmaɪn]	v. 逐渐削弱
communally	[kəˈmjuːnəli]	adv. 公有地，社区地
hierarchy	[ˈhaɪərɑːki]	n. 等级制度
prominent	[ˈprɒmɪnənt]	adj. 突出的，杰出的；突起的；著名的
allergy	[ˈælədʒi]	n.【医】过敏症
prioritize	[praɪˈɒrətaɪz]	vt. 按重要性排列，优先顺序；优先处理
rectangular	[rekˈtæŋɡjələ(r)]	adj. 矩形的
accessibility	[əkˌsesəˈbɪləti]	n. 易接近，可到达
flip	[flɪp]	vt. 快速翻转
decline	[dɪˈklaɪn]	v. 婉拒
hospitality	[ˌhɒspɪˈtæləti]	n. 殷勤好客；招待，款待

 Part IV Viewing

Do You Really Understand Chopsticks?

Watch a short video and fill in the blanks.

Food culture has witnessed the process of human _____. _____, in its own way, shows the connection between people and food. Chopsticks are equally sized and we usually call them _____. Why?

Chopsticks reveal the traditional Chinese concept of _____. There are some taboos associated with chopsticks and all of them reflect _____ to others.

Chopsticks have one _____ end and one _____ end. This traditional design fully and perfectly reflects the people-oriented ideology. Standard chopsticks are 7.6 Chinese inches long to represent people's seven _____ and six sensory pleasures, which reflect the essential difference between humans and animals.

Chinese ancestors advocated _____ and _____ between humans and nature, and carried out this idea in selecting the material for chopsticks. Chopsticks are usually made from precious natural wood. Ebony is stable and it is very _____ for the human body and very _____ for making chopsticks. A pair of chopsticks not only picks up food to feed hungry stomachs, but also picks up the gift and love that ancestors gave to their _____.

Part V Practising

Translation.

Translate the paragraphs into English or Chinese.

到北京旅游，必须做两件事：一件是登长城；另一件是吃北京烤鸭。闻名遐迩的北京烤鸭曾仅供于宫廷，而现在北京数百家餐厅均有供应。

北京烤鸭源于600年前的明朝。来自全国各地的厨师被选出来到京城为皇帝做饭。人们认为在皇宫做饭是一种莫大的荣誉，只有厨艺出众者才能获得这份工作。事实上，正是这些宫廷厨师使北京烤鸭的烹饪艺术日臻完善。

Chopsticks are usually made of wood or bamboo, and used for eating

Asian food. It is believed that chopsticks were developed over 5,000 years ago in China. The earliest evidence of a pair of chopsticks made out of bronze was excavated from the Ruins of Yin near Anyang, Henan Province, dating back to roughly 1200 BC. Chopsticks are so frequently used in daily life that they have become more than a kind of tableware and have fostered a set of etiquette and customs of their own.

Writing.

How would you introduce Chinese food to foreigners? Please try to write a composition of at least 120 words.

Unit 11

Dunhuang Frescoes

Learning Objectives

After learning this unit, you will be able to:
- learn the basic information about Dunhuang frescoes, including words and expressions, proper names, etc;
- try to introduce murals in English;
- trace sources of relics protection.

Dunhuang fresco is the composing part of Dunhuang Mogao Caves grotto art. The Mogao Caves, also known as the Caves of the Thousand Buddhas, is a system of 492 temples 25 kilometers southeast of the center of Dunhuang, an oasis strategically located at a religious and cultural crossroads on the Silk Road, in Gansu province, northwestern China. The caves contain some of the finest examples of Buddhist art spanning a period of 1,000 years.

Dunhuang frescoes have abundant contents, varied forms and vivid time characteristics. They show that the craftsmen at that time had advanced painting skills and abundant imagination power. They provide a large number of objective materials for research on Chinese art history.

Dunhuang fresco art is one of the essences of traditional Chinese culture and plays an extremely important role in our traditional cultural heritage. It is a huge Chinese treasure trove of art, whether the size, quantity or content is vast and colorful. In the face of the colorful Dunhuang frescoes, we cannot help but be deeply attracted by their diversity of the form and rich picture.

Part 1 Lead-in

*Watch a short video of **Dunhuang Frescoes** and discuss the following questions.*

- What did people carve on rocks some 10,000 years ago?
- What animal did the ancient painter draw on the wall and become alive according to the legend?
- Why did Dunhuang frescoes on the subject of religion rapidly develop all of a sudden?
- What stories do Dunhuang Mogao Caves tell us?

Part II Reading

Dunhuang

The city of Dunhuang, in northwest China, is situated at a point of vital **strategic** and **logistical** importance, on a crossroads of two major trade routes within the Silk Road network. Lying in an **oasis** at the edge of the **Taklamakan Desert**, Dunhuang was one of the first trading cities encountered by **merchants** arriving in China from the west. It was also an ancient site of **Buddhist** religious activity,

strategic
[strə'tiːdʒɪk]
adj. 战略的；战略性的

logistical
[lə'dʒɪstɪkl] adj. 物流的

oasis [əʊ'eɪsɪs] n. 绿洲

Taklamakan Desert
塔克拉玛干沙漠

merchant
['mɜːtʃənt] n. 商人；进出口批发商

Buddhist
['bʊdɪst] n. 佛教徒

中国传统文化英语谈

pilgrim ['pɪlgrɪm]
n. 朝觐者；朝圣的人

garrison ['gærɪsn]
n. 守备部队；要塞；驻防地

Mogao Caves 莫高窟

depositary
[dɪ'pɒzɪtəri] n. 储藏所

millennium
[mɪ'lenɪəm] n. 一千年；千禧年

vibrant ['vaɪbrənt]
adj. 充满活力的；生机勃勃的

hub [hʌb] n. 中心；轮轴

junction ['dʒʌŋkʃn]
n. 交叉路口，汇合处，枢纽站

and was a popular destination for **pilgrims**, as well as acting as a **garrison** town protecting the region. The remarkable **Mogao Caves**, a collection of 492 caves in the cliffs to the south of the city, contain the largest **depositary** of historical documents along the Silk Roads and bear witness to the cultural, religious, social and commercial activity that took place in Dunhuang across the first **millennium**. The city changed hands many times over its long history, but remained a **vibrant hub** of exchange until the 11th century, after which its role in Silk Road trade began to decline.

The Silk Road routes from China to the west passed to the north and south of the Taklamakan Desert, and Dunhuang lay at the **junction** where these two routes came together. Additionally, the city lies near the western edge of the Gobi Desert, and north of the Mingsha Sand Dunes, making Dunhuang a vital resting point for merchants and

pilgrims traveling through the region from all directions. As such, Dunhuang played a key role in the passage of the Silk Road trade to and from China, and over the course of the first **millennium** AD, it was one of the most important cities to grow up on these routes. Dunhuang **initially** acted as a garrison town protecting the region and its trade routes, and a **commandery** was established there in the 2nd century BC by the Chinese Han dynasty (206 BC−220 AD). A number of ancient passes, such as the Yu Guan or "Jade Gate" and the Yang Guan, or "Southern Gate", illustrate the strategic importance of the city and its position on what amounted to a **medieval** highway across the deserts.

The history of this ancient Silk Road city is reflected in the Mogao Caves, also known as the Qianfodong (the Caves of the Thousand Buddhas), an astonishing collection of 492 caves that were dug into the cliffs just south of the city. The first caves were founded in 366 AD by Buddhist monks, and distinguished Dunhuang as a center for Buddhist learning, drawing large numbers of pilgrims to the city. Monks and pilgrims often traveled via the Silk Roads, and indeed a number of religions, including Buddhism, spread into areas around the trading routes in this way.

The Mogao Caves illustrate not only the religious importance of Dunhuang, but also its significance as a center of cultural and commercial exchange. One of the caves, known as the "library cave", contains as many as 40,000 scrolls, a depositary of documents that is of enormous value in understanding the cultural diversity of this Silk Road city. The earliest text is dated to 405 AD, while the latest dates to

initially [ɪˈnɪʃəli] adv. 开始；最初；起初

commandery [kəˈmɑːndəri] n. 封地

medieval [ˌmediˈiːvl] adj. 中世纪的

deliberately
[dɪˈlɪbərətli] adv.
有意地；从容地；
不慌不忙地

monastery
[ˈmɒnəstri] n. 修
道院；寺庙

recipient [rɪˈsɪpiənt]
n. 接受者

ceramics
[sɪˈræmɪks] n. 陶
瓷制品；陶器

embroidery
[ɪmˈbrɔɪdəri] n.
刺绣；刺绣品

1002 AD. The arrangement of documents in this library cave suggests that they were **deliberately** stored there, and it seems that the local **monasteries** used the cave as a storage room. They provide a picture of Dunhuang as a vibrant hub of Silk Road trade, and give an indication of the range of goods that were exchanged in the city. According to these documents, a large number of imports arrived from as far away as north-east Europe. Dunhuang was not simply a **recipient** of trade, but had a very active export market too.

The scrolls refer to a large number of goods that were produced in the city and its surrounding regions and sold to merchants, including silks of many varieties, cotton, wool, fur, tea, **ceramics**, medicine, fragrances, jade, camels, sheep, dye, dried fruits, tools, and **embroidery**. This unique view of the imports and exports from the markets of Dunhuang illustrates the vibrancy of the Silk Road trade along the routes into western China.

Reading Comprehension.

Choose the best answer according to the text.

1. Which location description of Dunhuang is wrong?

    A. It's on a crossroads of two major trade routes.

    B. It's in the Taklamakan Desert.

    C. It was one of the first trading cities met by foreign businessmen.

    D. It's in north-west China.

2. When did Dunhuang's role in the Silk Road trade begin to decline?

    A. In the 11th century.

    B. During the first millennium.

C. In the 2nd century BC.

D. In 366 AD.

3. Which was **NOT** the key role of Dunhuang?

    A. A vital resting point for merchants and pilgrims.

    B. A key role in the passage of the Silk Road trade to and from Central Asia.

    C. A garrison town protecting the region and its trade routes.

    D. The position of a medieval highway across the deserts.

4. What is the length from the earliest text to the latest text?

    A. About 400 years.

    B. About 500 years.

    C. About 600 years.

    D. About 700 years.

5. Which belongs to the goods that were produced in the city and its surrounding regions and then sold to merchants?

    A. Spice.

    B. Gem.

    C. Poultry.

    D. Tools.

Work in groups to discuss the following questions.

- Do you prefer travel destinations with natural scenery or rich history?
- Could you recite the vital position of Dunhuang on the Silk Road?
- Why did Dunhuang's role in Silk Road begin to decline gradually?
- Do you think Dunhuang is able to help to revive travel on the old Silk Road apart from its historical and cultural relics?
- Have you ever been to any other ancient cities all around our country? And try to recall them.

Fan Jinshi: Daughter of Dunhuang

[A] The Mogao Caves in Dunhuang, China, began to be built during the **reign** of Emperor Fu Jian (338–385) of one of the 16 kingdoms in northern China. After construction spanning several dynasties, a **sprawling** structure was formed, including 735 caves, with 45,000 square meters of **murals**, and 2,415 clay-painted sculptures which are of extremely high artistic value. The Mogao Caves were listed as a world cultural **heritage** by UNESCO in 1987.

[B] The art treasures of the Mogao Caves have captivated generations of people, and it has also brought them to forge an **indissoluble** bond with Dunhuang. Among them, Fan Jinshi, former president and current honorary president of the Dunhuang Academy, the institution responsible for the conservation, management, and research of these grottoes, is an illustrative one.

[C] Speaking of her ties with Dunhuang, Fan described it as "accidental". She went to Dunhuang in 1962 for the first time. Arranged by the school, Fan and three classmates went to the Dunhuang Institute of Cultural Relics (now Dunhuang Academy) to do some fieldwork. The institute in her imagination, was supposed to be "a romantic and elegant place". However, she was **dumbfounded** when she arrived there. The staff members there were all **emaciated** with **sallow** complexions and wore clothes that had faded from being washed many times. But as soon as she entered the cave and gazed at the vivid, **mesmerizing** murals on the walls, Fan was immediately amazed by its artistic beauty.

[D] Considering the hardships of the environment, Fan's parents worried that their daughter, who had grown up in a relatively comfortable environment in the city, would not be able to endure these hardships, and thus opposed her working in Dunhuang. They eventually had to give in as she insisted on heading there. Before leaving, her father told her that since it was her own choice, she should give her best. "My father's words made me acknowledge the onset of maturity. One must have no regrets about one's choices", said Fan.

[E] The extremely difficult environment was quite challenging for Fan to acclimatize to, resulting in the deterioration of her health. Many people

---

dumbfound ['dʌm'faʊnd] v. 使……惊呆

emaciated [ɪ'meɪsɪeɪtɪd] v. 消瘦；使衰弱 adj. 憔悴的；虚弱的

sallow ['sæləʊ] adj. 灰黄的；蜡黄的

mesmerizing ['mezməraɪzɪŋ] adj. 有吸引力的；有魅力的

asthma ['æsmə] *n.* 气喘；哮喘

retention [rɪ'tenʃn] *n.* 保留；维持

working there began to suffer from **asthma** and dirt **retention** in the lungs. However, when faced with this unforgiving environment, Fan resolutely chose to persevere. From mural disease control to cliff reinforcement, from environmental monitoring to sand control, Fan fulfilled her original aspiration and mission in all areas of Dunhuang preservation.

[F] In 1998, Fan, who was 60 years old at the time, rose to the rank of president of Dunhuang Academy. Soon after taking office, many people proposed to make Mogao Caves listed and commercialized to promote tourism and boost western China's economy.

ancestor ['ænsestə(r)] *n.* 祖宗；祖先

[G] Fan firmly disagreed. "The protection of cultural relics is a very complicated thing. What if they ruin this cultural heritage? There is only one Mogao Caves in the world." She believes that it is her responsibility to protect the heritage left by the **ancestors**. "If the Mogao Caves are destroyed, then I will be remembered as a **sinner** in history."

[H] Thanks to the efforts of Fan and her colleagues, the charm of Dunhuang has become increasingly visible and accessible to the world. With the increasing popularity of the region, the Mogao Caves have gradually attracted more and more attention from home and abroad. However, a new problem emerged—the number of tourists to Dunhuang soared to over 200,000 every year. Once, Fan **sneezed** due to the overwhelming fragrance of perfume when she was inspecting a cave. She realized that the murals are difficult to preserve and will continue to erode over time, and the **corrosion** of the murals by breathing, sweating, and **aerosols** from the increasing number of tourists **exacerbates** this process. Compared with the state of the murals 100 years ago, the colors have faded a lot, and the increasingly blurred murals worried her. "If tourists are prohibited from visiting and this treasure of mankind is sealed off, it would be quite a selfish act", was the dilemma confronting Fan.

[I] After conducting a great deal of research and discussion on how to protect the cultural relics and **alleviate** the impact of excessive tourism on the murals and colored sculptures, the Dunhuang Academy began to build a visitor service center in early 2003. At the center, visitors could obtain a **comprehensive** understanding of the cultural features, historical background, and

sinner [ˈsɪnə(r)] n. 罪人

sneeze [sniːz] v. 打喷嚏

corrosion [kəˈrəʊʒn] n. 腐蚀；侵蚀

aerosol [ˈeərəsɒl] n. 气溶胶

exacerbate [ɪɡˈzæsəbeɪt] vi. 加剧；使恶化；使加重

alleviate [əˈliːvieɪt] vt. 减轻；缓和；缓解

comprehensive [ˌkɒmprɪˈhensɪv] adj. 综合的

cave composition of the grottoes through film, virtual tours, and exhibitions before entering the cave, and then be taken into the cave by a professional guide for further field visits.

glean [gli:n] vt. 收集；四处搜集

[J] "This not only allows tourists to **glean** more detailed cultural information in a shorter period of time, but also greatly eases the huge pressure on the preservation efforts of the Mogao Caves caused by excessive numbers of tourists", said Fan.

[K] Fan also proposed establishing a "digital Dunhuang"— making high-resolution digital images of caves, murals, colored sculptures, and all other cultural relics. Meanwhile, Dunhuang's documents, research results, and related materials scattered around the world would be integrated into electronic files. "The murals are cultural relics that cannot be regenerated, nor are they eternal." This prompted Fan to consider using "digitalization" to permanently preserve them. With a panoramic tour, everyone can take in the magnificent details of Mogao Caves at close range. To a certain extent, this is an experience that provides richness and **intimacy** not possible on a crowded visit to the site itself.

intimacy ['ɪntɪməsi] *n.* 亲密；密切

[L] After years of hard work, "Digital Dunhuang" was officially launched in 2016. Visitors to the website could now view a high-definition **panorama** of the 30 classic caves for free with just a click of the mouse, and it was almost as good as visiting the site in person. This not only satiates their desire to visit the Mogao Caves, but also reduces the damage caused by excessive tourism.

panorama [ˌpænəˈrɑːmə] *n.* 全景；综合画卷

[M] Fan's contribution in promoting the preservation of Dunhuang has also been **unanimously** recognized by the academic community. Ji Xianlin, a famous academic expert in China, once praised Fan with one word: **meritorious**. This word suffices to explain her great contribution, and it is also a true portrayal of her achievements in protecting Dunhuang's cultural relics.

unanimously [juː(ː)ˈnænɪməsli] *adv.* 全体一致地

meritorious [ˌmerɪˈtɔːriəs] *adj.* 值得赞扬的

[N] Fan, who is now 83 years old, is still devoting much of her time and effort to protecting Dunhuang's splendid cultural heritage. Her life and career have been dedicated to Dunhuang and the cause of national cultural relic protection.

New Phrases	
be of high value	价值很高
forge a bond	建立联系
fade from	从……逐渐消失
give in	屈服；让步；认输
insist on	坚持；强调
acclimatize to	适应
take office	就职；任职
seal off	封闭；封锁
integrate into	融入；与……成为一体
take in	欣赏；观看，领悟
as good as	几乎；差不多
dedicate to	献身于；把时间和精力用于

Reading Comprehension.

In this section, you are going to read ten statements attached to the above passage. Each statement contains information given in one of the paragraphs. Identify the paragraph from which the information is derived. You may choose a paragraph more than once. Each paragraph is marked with a letter.

1. The Dunhuang Academy began to build a visitor service center in the early 2003._____
2. Fan's parents worried that their daughter would not be able to endure the difficulties, and thus didn't agree with her working in Dunhuang._____
3. The Mogao Caves were listed as a world cultural heritage by UNESCO in 1987._____
4. Ji Xianlin once praised Fan with the word meritorious._____
5. Some people put forward to make Mogao Caves commercialized to promote

local tourism and the economy. _____

6. Fan's whole life and career have been dedicated to Dunhuang and the cause of national cultural relic protection. _____
7. Dunhuang has become increasingly popular and attractive to the world due to the efforts of Fan and her colleagues. _____
8. Many staff working in Dunhuang suffer from asthma and lung diseases, including Fan. _____
9. At first, Fan thought Dunhuang was romantic and elegant, but she was astonished when she arrived there. _____
10. After years of hard work, "Digital Dunhuang" was officially launched in 2016. _____

Work in groups to discuss the following questions.

- How do you understand the craftsman spirit of Chinese scholars and experts? And try to introduce them in native English.
- Try to retell and comment on the life story of Fan Jinshi with your team members.

 Part III Listening and Speaking

News report.

New Words	
heavy-duty	*adj.* 严肃的
controversial	*adj.* 有争议的
crucified	*v.* 严惩；折磨

续表

New Words	
loom	*vi.* 赫然耸现；逼近
rifle	*n.* 步枪；来复枪
trafficked	*v.* 通行；交易；买卖
narrative	*n.* 叙述；叙事
indigenous	*adj.* 当地的；土生土长的
property	*n.* 所有物；不动产

In this section, you will hear an introduction to city murals. Try to understand it and finish the following questions.

1. Who created the mural?

    A. Kent Twitchell.　　　　　　　　B. Steve McQueen.

    C. Leslie Rainer.　　　　　　　　　D. David Alfaro Siqueiros.

2. Why did Kent Twitchell begin to paint?

    A. He regarded himself a modernist artist.

    B. He fancied some actors and actresses.

    C. He felt good through painting.

    D. He would become famous through painting.

3. How could you describe the mural from 1932 by Mexican artist David Alfaro Siqueiros?

    A. Optimistic.　　　　　　　　　　B. Controversial.

    C. Humorous.　　　　　　　　　　D. Scary.

4. What is the national symbol bird of the United States?

    A. Sparrow.　　　　　　　　　　　B. Robin.

    C. Pigeon.　　　　　　　　　　　　D. Eagle.

5. What do an African woman of the Masai tribe and native birds of Kenya represent?
   A. The future's prosperity.
   B. The poverty in Africa.
   C. The difficult life of the local peoples.
   D. The humanitarian help from UNICEF.

Listen again and decide whether the following statements are true (T) or false (F).

1. The city murals add pollution to the city. _____
2. It's hard to find the hidden murals everywhere. _____
3. Some important murals have been painted over or damaged. _____
4. Local leaders appreciated the image of the eagle. _____
5. Artist Lydia Emily says her work shows the face of a young woman named Jessica and a bird that represents chains and prison. _____
6. Officials recently eased rules about street murals in an effort to get more art and color in the city. _____

Work in groups to discuss the following questions.

- What are the roles of murals in city design and decoration?
- What are the deep meanings behind each mural mentioned in the passage?
- What do you know about the differences between Chinese and western murals? What about in your hometown?

Spot Dictation.

New Words		
surrender	[səˈrendə(r)]	v. 放弃；投降
cuneiform	[ˈkjuːnɪfɔːm]	n. 楔形文字
archaeological	[ˌɑːkɪəˈlɒdʒɪkəl]	a. 考古的

Listen to the following passage and fill in the blanks with the exact words or phrases you hear.

  United States officials say an American company has agreed to surrender thousands of ancient artifacts from the Middle East. The company also agreed to pay a $3 million fine to the government. Federal (1) _____ accused Hobby Lobby, a business specializing in arts and crafts, of illegally importing artifacts into the country. The government lawyers said in a (2) _____ that Hobby Lobby paid $1.6 million in 2010 for over 5,000 earthen tablets and other objects. Many of the artifacts have examples of cuneiform, one of the earliest known systems of writing. The artifacts and other objects purchased were sent to several Hobby Lobby stores. The shipments were (3) _____ as coming from Turkey and Israel. The shipments were also said to contain samples of "ceramic tiles" or (4) "_____".

  Federal prosecutors said an expert warned the company that the artifacts were likely stolen from archaeological areas in Iraq. Importing Iraqi cultural property into the United States has been (5) _____ since 2004, the statement said. Under Iraqi law, all antiquities found in the country are considered the property of the state. (6) _____ cannot own them without permission from the Iraqi government.

The president of Hobby Lobby, Steve Green, said the company has (7) _____ with the U.S. government. He also said that the company should have "more carefully questioned" how the objects got into the country.

Green said Hobby Lobby did not purchase any items directly from (8) _____ in Iraq. He said the company had worked with dealers in the United Arab Emirates. He also said that Hobby Lobby (9) "_____" such acts and has always acted with the aim of protecting "ancient items of cultural and his historical importance".

On Thursday, "Hobby Lobby" trended worldwide on Twitter and Facebook. One writer said: "Hobby Lobby (10) _____ Iraq was not a story I was expecting, but then again this is 2017." The company has agreed to develop a new policy for buying cultural property. It has also agreed to provide reports to the government about such (11) _____ for 18 months.

Hobby Lobby began starting a collection of historical Bibles and other artifacts in 2009. Its owners are known for having strong Christian beliefs.

Green himself owns one of the world's largest collections of (12) _____ . He is building a Museum of the Bible in Washington, D.C. The building is set to open later this year.

And that's what's trending today. I'm Dan Friedell.

Part IV Practising

Read the following passage and choose the correct word from the following answers.

A. communication	G. oasis
B. marked	H. cultural
C. dialog	I. history
D. witness	J. mingling

E. exchange	K. ancient
F. harmoniously	L. wheat

More than 2,000 years ago, the ancient Silk Road was opened to (1) _____ goods between the East and the West, which traversed from China's ancient capital Chang'an all the way to (2) _____ Rome. The trade route (3) _____ the beginning of a new era for human exchanges. Caravans from different countries carried goods like silk, spices, jewels, (4) _____ and grapes, and traded with each other through the ancient Silk Road. It was also a road of (5) _____ between China and many other countries in the world. People got along, respected and learned from each other. It led to a (6) _____ of different kinds of societies, economies, lifestyles and cultures. It also contributed to the prosperity of the (7) _____ city Dunhuang in northwest China. As a major stop on the ancient Silk Road, Dunhuang was a trade hub and a center of (8) _____ exchanges. Here, people of different nations and religions lived together (9) _____ . With the ancient Silk Road, Dunhuang became one of China's most prosperous cities. Many of the Silk Road stories were painted into frescoes in Dunhuang, which stood (10) _____ to the vicissitudes of the times.

Translation.

Translate the following paragraphs into English or Chinese.

敦煌莫高窟（Dunhuang Mogao Caves）坐落于中国西部甘肃省。这些石窟刻于距离敦煌东南方向25千米处鸣沙山的悬崖上。敦煌莫高窟是规模最大、保存时间最长的佛教艺术宝库，现存735个洞窟，壁画（frescoes）4万5千多平方米。这些壁画展现了佛（Buddha）的形象和活动以及人与神之间的关系。敦煌壁画中的舞蹈人物是全人类的一颗璀璨的宝石。敦煌莫高窟在 1987 年被列入世界遗产名录（World Heritage List）。

Dunhuang is a renowned tourist resort famous for the Mogao Caves. In ancient times, Dunhuang was the center of trade between China and its western neighbors. With the flourishing of trade along the Silk Road, Dunhuang quickly developed to become the most open area in international trade in Chinese history. Over 1,000 caves were cut out of cliffs in Dunhuang. The caves reflect the Silk Road civilization and important aspects of Chinese people's religious life, art, and customs in history, including the introduction of Buddhism to China during this period. Dunhuang grottoes have always been regarded as the national treasure of China.

Writing.

If your American friend Mike wants to visit China, write an article to introduce Dunhuang in English to him.

Unit 12

Traditional Chinese Medicine

Learning Objectives

After learning this unit, you will be able to:
- learn the basic information about some traditional Chinese medicine including words and expressions, proper names, etc;
- try to introduce Traditional Chinese Medicine in English;
- trace sources of Chinese medicine.

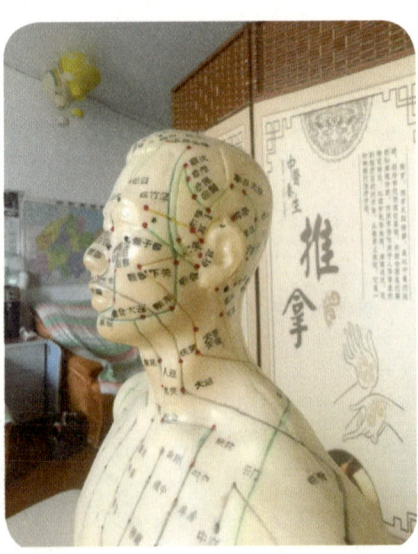

Traditional Chinese Medicine (TCM) is thousands of years old and has changed little over the centuries. Its basic concept is that a vital force of life, called *qi*, surges through the body. Any imbalance in *qi* can cause disease and illness. This imbalance is most commonly thought to be caused by an alteration in the opposite and complementary forces that make up the *qi*. These are called *yin* and *yang*. Ancient Chinese believed that humans are microcosms of the larger surrounding universe, and are interconnected with nature and subject to its forces. The balance between health and disease is a key concept. TCM treatment seeks to restore this balance through treatment specific to the individual. It is believed that to regain balance, you must achieve the balance between the internal body organs and the external elements of earth, fire, water, wood, and metal.

Part I Lead-in

*Watch a short video clip of **Traditional Chinese Medicine** and discuss the following questions.*

- Why was the whole world rejoicing for Tu Youyou?
- What principles does TCM follow?
- How many countries and districts has TCM spread to all over the world?
- What kinds of medical treatments does the speaker mention according to the video clip?

Part II Reading

Yin-Yang in Traditional Chinese Medicine

Just like **rationalism** forms the basis for Western medicine, the Taoist philosophy of *yin-yang* forms the basis for Traditional Chinese Medicine (TCM). While many people have heard the term *yin-yang* or know its famous symbol, few understand what *yin-yang* truly is, and even fewer people know how it relates to Traditional Chinese Medicine.

In Chinese philosophy, *yin-yang*, which translates into "dark-bright", describes the notion that everything in nature consists of two **paradoxical** phases or energies.

In TCM, the concept of *yin* and *yang* serves as the foundation for understanding health, as well as **diagnosing** and treating illnesses. *Yin-yang* is first referenced in the *Book of Changes*, which was written around 700 BC. According to it, all phenomena are composed of two opposite, but mutually **interconnected** forces, known as *yin* and *yang*.

To better understand the concepts of *yin* and *yang*, it helps to know about their Four Aspects. The Four Aspects describe the relationship between *yin* and *yang*. *Yin* and *yang* are **simultaneous**:

Opposites—*Yin* and *yang* are opposites. A common *yin* and *yang* relationship is day and night. While opposites, they can only be understood as a relationship. For example, darkness is relative to *yin*, while *yang* is relative to light. The balance between the two is always shifting and progressing in a **cyclical** fashion.

Interdependent—While opposites, *yin* and *yang* are interdependent. One cannot exist without the other. *Yin* and *yang* are **mutually** dependent on each other. One cannot exist without the other. Everything that has *yin*, must have yang, and **vice versa**.

Mutually **Transformative**—*Yin* and *yang* are constantly in a state of flux and affect each other. If one changes, the other follows. Nature, by definition, cannot be **static**. Just as a state of total *yin* is reached, *yang* begins to grow. For example, there is no day without night.

Mutually Consuming—*Yin* and *yang* are naturally balanced, but are continuously changing. The change is typically harmonious, but can become imbalanced. There are four possible states of imbalance:

★ Excess of *Yin*

★ Excess of *Yang*

★ Deficiency of *Yin*

★ Deficiency of *Yang*

In terms of the human body, *yin* is associated with the lower parts of the body, while *yang* is associated with the upper body and back. Given *yin* and *yang*'s interconnectivity, diseases are not seen as entities separate from the body, but instead are understood as states of *yin* and *yang* imbalance.

In traditional Chinese medicine, this interconnectivity is understood as a group of four opposites, collectively known as the Eight Principles. The table below shows the inverse relationship of *yin-yang*.

cyclical ['saɪklɪkəl] *adj.* 周期性；周期的，循环的

mutually ['mjuːtʃuəli] *adj.* 相互地；彼此；共同地

vice versa *adv.* 反之亦然

transformative [træns'fɔːmətɪv] *adj.* 有改革能力的

static ['stætɪk] *adj.* 静止的，静态的，停滞的

The Eight Principles

Yin	Yang
Exterior	Interior
Deficiency (Xu)	Excess (Shi)
Cold	Heat

Yin and *yang* are in constant **flux**. If one becomes unbalanced in the body, illness occurs. For example, since *yin* is cold, an excess of *yin* can cause illnesses such as **insomnia** and dry mouth. Conversely, a *yang* deficiency can cause cold limbs and a sickly **complexion**. Good health then, is maintained by balancing *yin* and *yang*.

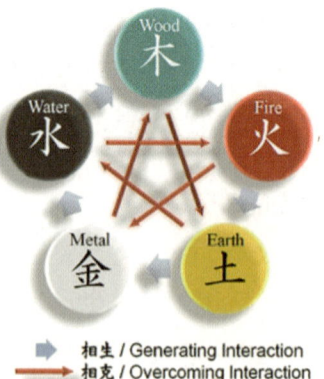

➡ 相生 / Generating Interaction
── 相克 / Overcoming Interaction

While the change of *yin* and *yang* may seem **random**, they actual follow a pattern known Xu Xing or the Five Phases, which shows how and when *yin* will shift to *yang* and vice versa. Typically, Xu Xing is used to describe the change of seasons and states of elements. For example, spring giving rise to early summer, which turns into late summer, which then becomes fall, then winter, then spring again.

Reading Comprehension.

Choose the best answer according to the text.

1. Which is **NOT** *yin* and *yang*'s function in traditional Chinese medicine?

    A. Understanding health.

    B. Forming rationalism.

    C. Diagnosing illness.

    D. Treating illness.

2. Which is **NOT** correct in describing the relationship between *yin* and *yang*?

    A. Opposite.

    B. Interdependent.

    C. Imbalanced.

    D. Mutually transformative and consuming.

3. In terms of the human body, what is *yin* associated with?

    A. The lower parts of the body.

    B. The upper parts of the body.

    C. The organs.

    D. The limbs.

4. According to the Eight Principles, what is the opposite of deficiency?

    A. Interior.   B. Excess.

    C. Heat.   D. Yang.

5. Which does **NOT** follow the Five Phases pattern?

    A. The sickly complexion.

    B. The change of *yin* and *yang*.

    C. The change of four seasons.

    D. The states of five elements.

Work in groups to discuss the following questions.

- Could you paraphrase the relationship between *yin* and *yang*?
- How does *yin-yang* form the basis for TCM?
- What will happen if there are states of imbalance?
- How do you understand the Eight Principles?
- Do you think TCM is a systematic system?

Acupuncture

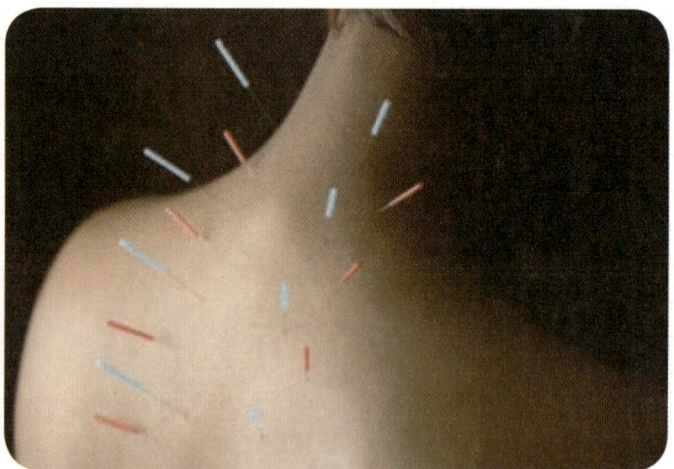

electrical current
[iˈlektrikəlˈkʌrənt]
n. 电流

Acupuncture is a technique in which practitioners insert fine needles into the skin to treat health problems. The needles may be manipulated manually or stimulated with small **electrical currents** (electro acupuncture). Acupuncture has been in use in some form for at least 2,500 years. It originated from Traditional Chinese Medicine but has gained popularity worldwide since the 1970s.

Traditional Chinese Medicine explains acupuncture as a technique for balancing the flow of energy or life force—known as chi or *qi* (chee)—believed to flow through pathways (**meridians**) in your body. By inserting needles into specific points along these meridians, acupuncture practitioners believe that your energy flow will re-balance.

It's primarily used to relieve pain but also has been used to treat other conditions. More than 3 million Americans use acupuncture, but it is even more popular in other countries. In France, for example, one in five people has tried acupuncture.

According to the World Health Organization, acupuncture is used in 103 of 129 countries that reported data. In the United States, data from the National Health Interview Survey showed a 50% increase in the number of acupuncture users between 2002 and 2012. In 2012, 6.4% of U.S. adults reported they had used acupuncture, and 1.7% reported they had used it in the past 12 months.

National survey data indicate that in the United States, acupuncture is most commonly used for pain, such as back, joint, or neck pain.

How acupuncture works?

Acupuncture seeks to release the flow of the body's vital energy or chi by stimulating points along 14 energy pathways. Some scientists believe that the needles cause the body to release **endorphins**—natural painkillers—and may boost blood flow and change brain activity. **Skeptics** say acupuncture works only because people believe it will, an effect called the **placebo** effect.

Studies in animals and people, including studies that used imaging methods to see what's happening in the brain, have shown that acupuncture may affect nervous system function.

Acupuncture may have direct effects on the **tissues** where the needles are inserted. This type of effect has been seen in connective tissue.

Acupuncture has nonspecific effects (effects due to incidental aspects of a treatment rather than its main **mechanism** of action). Nonspecific effects may be due to the patient's belief in the treatment, the relationship between the practitioner and the patient, or other factors not directly caused by the insertion of needles. In many studies, the benefit of acupuncture has been greater when it was compared with no treatment than when it was compared with **sham** (simulated or fake) acupuncture procedures, such as the use of a device that **pokes** the skin but does not penetrate it.

These findings suggest that nonspecific effects contribute to the beneficial effect of acupuncture on pain or other symptoms.

Research has shown that acupuncture may be helpful for several pain conditions, including back or neck pain, knee pain associated with **osteoarthritis**, and postoperative pain. It may also help relieve joint pain associated with the use of **aromatase inhibitors**, which are drugs used in people with breast cancer.

An analysis of data from 20 studies (6,376 participants) of people with painful conditions (back pain, osteoarthritis, neck pain, or headaches) showed that the beneficial effects of acupuncture continued for a year after the end of treatment for all conditions except neck pain.

Does acupuncture hurt?

Acupuncture needles are very thin, and most people feel no pain or very little pain when they are inserted. They often say they feel energized or relaxed after the treatment. However, the needles can cause temporary soreness.

Although acupuncture is generally safe and serious problems are rare, there are some risks. Needles that are not **sterile** can cause **infection**. Make sure that your practitioner uses sterile needles that are thrown away after one use. In some acupuncture points, needles inserted too deeply can puncture the lungs or **gallbladder** or cause problems with your blood **vessels**. That is why it is important to use a practitioner who is well-trained in acupuncture.

sterile ['steraɪl] adj. 无菌的；无效果的
infection [ɪn'fekʃn] n.〈医〉传染，感染
gallbladder ['gɔːl,blædə] n. 胆囊
vessel ['vesl] n. 血管

Read the text and decide whether the following statements are true (T) or false (F).

1. Acupuncture originated from Traditional Chinese Medicine and are widely used for at least 2,500 years. _____
2. Acupuncture can help balance the energy and chi through meridians in your body. _____
3. Acupuncture is only used to relieve pain. _____
4. Acupuncture is used in more than 100 countries. _____
5. The needles cause the body to release endorphins, which may boost blood flow and change brain activity. _____
6. Nonspecific effects has no beneficial effect of acupuncture on pain or other symptoms. _____
7. There are no risks because acupuncture needles are very thin, and most people feel no pain or very little pain. _____
8. Practitioners should use sterile needles, or infection can be caused. _____

Part III Listening and Speaking

New Words and Phrases	
be accustomed to	习惯于做某事
chronic disease	慢性疾病
interrelated	相互关联（或影响）
strive to do sth.	努力做某事
wholesome	有益健康的
pharmaceutical market	制药市场
antibiotics	抗菌素；抗生素

In this section, you will hear an introduction to Chinese medicine. Try to understand it and finish the following questions.

1. Are Chinese people more accustomed to Chinese medicine?

    A. Yes.	B. No.

    C. It's hard to say.	D. Not mentioned.

2. Which area is one of the Chinese medicines' benefits?

    A. Acute disease.	B. Chronic disease.

    C. Incurable disease.	D. Mild disease.

3. Which is **NOT** one of the differences between Chinese and western medicines?

    A. Chinese medicine is based more on natural products while western medicine more on chemical products.

    B. Chinese medicine and western medicine had their own characteristics.

    C. Chinese medicine is more wholesome than western medicine.

    D. Chinese medicine is less wholesome than western medicine.

4. What pharmaceuticals are not included in TCM?

    A. Pathogens.	B. Antibodies.

    C. Antibiotics.	D. Genes.

5. What is the man's choice next time when he is sick probably?

　　A. Western medicine.　　　　B. Chinese medicine.

　　C. Integrative medicine.　　　D. Staying at home.

Listen again and decide whether the following statements are true (T) or false (F).

1. Chinese medicine believes that the different parts of the human body are all separated. _____

2. People consume more Chinese medicine than western medicine. _____

3. Chinese medicine represents only about 20%–25% of the whole pharmaceutical market. _____

4. Antibiotics can be harmful if they are taken too often. _____

5. Chinese medicine is not a cure-all. _____

Work in groups to discuss the following questions.

- What are the main curing fields of TCM?
- What are the primary differences between Chinese and Western medicines?
- What do you know about the role of TCM in the world?

Listen to the following passage and fill in the blanks with the exact words or phrases you hear.

　　The latest EU directive introduced a so-called simplified registration procedure for traditional herbal medicinal products to obtain a medical license.

　　Instead of going through safety tests and (1) _____ as regular chemical drugs, applicants are required to provide documents showing the herbal medicinal product is not harmful in the specified condition of use, as well as evidence that it has a (2) _____ of safe use, including 15 years in the EU.

Lin Bin, director of the Research and Development Institute of Traditional Chinese Medicine in Europe, says this requirement shuts out most Chinese (3) _____.

"Traditional Chinese medicine only entered the EU market (4) _____ in the 1990s, and they were (5) _____ as food supplement instead of medication. Therefore, there're few records of their medical use."

Obtaining such a license is estimated at between (6) _____ U.S. dollars per herb, scaring off many producers. However, the current situation is getting more complicated as the EU member states vary when it comes to the (7) _____ of the rules. The Netherlands, for instance, puts herbal products under the food category and there are loose restrictions. Lin Bin says traditional Chinese medicine will not be wiped out in the foreseeable future.

"The herbal medicines could still come in as food supplements, and after that, they could be sent to other EU countries in wholesale or retail. We had sent them to Germany, France and Italy." But he also (8) _____ this would not work in the UK.

The directive has been from (9) _____ many sides since it was adopted in 2004. The European Benefit Foundation and the Alliance for Natural Health recently (10) _____ to the European Court of Justice, the EU's highest judicial body, against the European Commission, demanding a revised legal framework for traditional herbal systems. So far, not a single Chinese traditional herbal medicinal product has been licensed. With over 2,000 years of history, the fate of traditional Chinese medicine remains unclear in Europe.

Part IV Viewing

Cupping Therapy Gains in Popularity at Home and Abroad

Remember the cupping marks on the swimming superstar Michael Phelps at the Rio Olympics? The shocking red marks opened people's eyes to Traditional Chinese Medicine (TCM) and the healing effects of cupping therapy used to ease muscle strain and soft tissue damage.

During the 2022 Winter Olympics, athletes from all over the world gathered in Beijing. The cupping therapy of the Traditional Chinese Medicine Health Center inside the Winter Olympic Village once again became a sensation among the athletes.

When applying cupping therapy, special cups are heated to create a vacuum and applied on specific acupoints or treatment sites. This method of negative pressure suction then produces a therapeutic effect.

Forms of cupping have been practiced for thousands of years in ancient Egypt, India, and China. Ancient artifacts dating back to the Spring and Autumn Period and Warring States Period in China show records of animal horns and negative thermal pressure techniques that were used to relieve pain and treat abscess blockages.

Cupping therapy has developed alongside TCM theory as a part of its strong foundation. TCM believes that the human body is associated with the dynamic balance of opposites in the form of *yin* and *yang*. Pain results from an imbalance in this unity within the body. TCM doctors believe that cupping allows for the decompression and decongestion of skin and tissues. Cupping therapy can effectively stimulate human meridians and acupoints, remove blockages in the body, detoxify the blood, and clear away heat to balance *yin* and *yang*.

In San Jose, TCM acupuncturist Dr. Li Ying treated an eczema patient who had suffered from eczema for more than four years and found no success using Western medicine. Then, through the recommendation of her cousin, the patient went to try out acupuncture and TCM.

Dr. Li Ying, a practitioner in California for 26 years, has witnessed the TCM medical practice transition from a source of suspicion to receiving recognition by local clients. Today, her clinic is well-known in California, and more and more clients are attracted to her practice through word of mouth about her medical skills.

Regarding the difference between Western medicine and TCM, she believes that the latter emphasizes holistic treatment to "treat both the symptoms and the root causes". TCM should guide those seeking treatment to better understand their diseases and ailments from various perspectives, including psychology and living habits, apart from relieving patients' pain. This is the unique perspective of TCM.

Due to the continued development of TCM, more and more Americans have come to recognize and accept the healthy treatment concept offered by TCM. At the same time, TCM practitioners continue to promote the treatment methods of TCM in every way possible, including through acupuncture, cupping, massages, Qigong, and Tai Chi, all in an attempt to prevent disease and improve fitness.

Work in groups and discuss the following questions.

- What's the difference between Western medicine and TCM?
- Do you know some treatment methods of TCM?
- What is the theory of TCM?

Part V Practising

Read the following passage and choose the correct word from the following answers.

A. increase	I. improvement
B. related	J. standard
C. proven	K. severe
D. effectively	L. disease
E. effective	M. deteriorating
F. fifth	N. shared
G. traditional	O. proportion
H. makeshift	

A total of 74,187 confirmed patients, which account for 91.5% of the total infections on the Chinese mainland, have been administered Traditional Chinese Medicine (TCM) as part of their treatment, and over 90% of them have shown (1) _____ during clinical observation, according to Yu Yanhong, a top official of the National Administration of Traditional Chinese

Medicine.

TCM has (2) _____ relieved symptoms, cut the rate of patients developing into (3) _____ conditions, raised the recovery rate, reduced the mortality rate and boosted patients' recovery, Yu said.

XuanfeiBaidu Granule can (4) _____ the lymphocyte recovery rate by 17% and the clinical cure rate by 22% in the controlled observation, according to Huang Luqi, an academician of the Chinese Academy of Engineering.

Liu Qingquan, head of the Beijing Hospital of Traditional Chinese Medicine, said that two TCM drugs-Jinhua Qinggan Granule and Lianhua Qingwen Capsule/Granule have (5) _____ to be effective in the treatment of mild COVID-19 cases, while Xuebijing Injection can help treat inflammation and coagulation dysfunction.

Zhang Boli, an academician of the Chinese Academy of Engineering, said that CM treatment has significantly lowered the (6) _____ of patients whose conditions turned from mild to severe. "None of the 564 patients at the TCM-oriented temporary hospital in Wuhan saw their health condition (7) _____ into severe", said Zhang. "We have therefore applied TCM treatment to over 10,000 patients in other (8) _____ hospitals, and the rate of patients developing into severe conditions was substantially reduced", said Zhang.

CM and Western medicine may come from two different medical systems and have different perspectives on health and diseases, but they are both based on the (9) _____ of factual clinical efficacy.

The practice of treating COVID-19 patients has proved once again that the precious wisdom left by our TCM ancestors is still practical, effective and economical. We would love to share these valuable experiences and (10) _____ treatment methods with all countries.

Translation.

Translate the following paragraphs into English or Chinese.

中医是世界医学的遗产。中医有比西方医学更好的治病方法。因为中医的效果和医治方式，中医在世界上越来越流行了。中医起源于古代，已经发展了很长一段时间，它收集了治疗不同疾病的各种方法。传统中医讲究人们身体系统的平衡。这就是说，一旦人的身体系统平衡，疾病就会消失。身体系统的损害是疾病的根源。

For more than five thousand years Chinese doctors have used needles to fight illness. This kind of medicine is called acupuncture. The doctor studies the sick person carefully. Then he puts needles into that person's body at the right places for his illness. Chinese doctors believe that they can control the body's natural forces in this way. At first, doctors in the West thought that this was just another kind of magic. Recently, however, they have found out that it is possible to cure many illnesses like this because the needles help the body to produce its own "medicines". In this way the body cures itself.

Nowadays doctors can do a lot of wonderful things. They can use thousands of medicines. They can give you pills and injections. They can even give you mechanical legs or a new heart. Sometimes modern medicine works like magic. But there are still a lot of illnesses that drugs and machines cannot cure completely. Medicine is not only a science; it is an art, too. And in the art of medicine, the mind is very important. You will not have a healthy body unless you have a healthy mind.

Writing.

If you are Li Hua, your New Zealand friend Lucy plans to come to China to study Traditional Chinese Medicine and send you an email to ask you about Traditional Chinese Medicine. Please reply to the email, including:

1. Welcome;

2. Brief introduction to TCM;

3. Express your best wishes.

References and Websites

1. Beijing Tourism. The Meaning of Ren in Confucianism[EB/OL].(2013-04-19)[2021-01-10].https://english.visitbeijing.com.cn/article/47OMqqdYK2e.

2. Catherine He. Dragon Boat Festival[EB/OL].(2021-01-27)[2021-01-15]. https://www.travelchinaguide.com/essential/holidays/dragon-boat.htm.

3. China Culture. Why we love Chinese kung fu[Z/OL].(2021-06-25)[2022-03-15].https://www.youtube.com/watch?v=ZmZpysU5ThM.

4. China Culture. Festive China: Lantern Festival[Z/OL].(2021-02-26)[2021-01-10].https://www.youtube.com/watch?v=kFQKWYGZNlE.

5. Festive China: The romantic story behind China's Valentine's Day[Z/OL].(2022-08-04)[2022-09-10].https://enapp.chinadaily.com.cn/a/202108/14/AP611734e9a310f03332fa799a.html.

6. Confucius[EB/OL].(2020-03-11)[2021-01-15].http://www.chinadaily.com.cn/m/shandong/shandongculture/2020-03/11/content_21626725.htm.

7. COLUMBIA UNIVERSITY. CONFUCIAN TEACHING[EB/OL].http://afe.easia.columbia.edu/at/conf_teaching/ct01.html.

8. Confucius philosophy quoted by foreign dignitaries[EB/OL].(2014-09-28)[2021-01-15].https://www.chinadaily.com.cn/culture/2014-09-28/content_18674682.htm.

9. Chinese plus. Chinses Historical and Cultural Figures 中国历史文化名人【英文版】[Z/OL].(2021-08-03)[2021-01-15].https://www.youtube.com/watch?v=yChAK_FcX9E.

10. Introduction to Wudang Taoism;Taoism;Wudang kungfu schools;Taiji Sword of Wudang Mountain;Wudang Inner School Boxing[EB/OL].(2011-07-11)[2022-03-15].http://www.chinadaily.com.cn/m/wudang/2011-07/11/content_12879639.htm.

11. Confucius[EB/OL].(2020-03-11)[2021-01-15].http://www.chinadaily.com.cn/m/shandong/shandongculture/2020-03/11/content_21626725.htm.

12. Confucius philosophy quoted by foreign dignitaries[EB/OL].(2014-09-28)[2021-01-15].https://www.chinadaily.com.cn/culture/2014-09/28/content_18674682.htm.

13. China Cultural Center in Brussels. Chinese Ink Painting[EB/OL].(2020-06-19)[2022-02-10].https://www.youtube.com/watch?v=wIpLzItqCqk.

14. Catharina Cheung. A look into the history & culture of Chinese opera.[EB/OL].(2020-06-29)[2022-02-25].https://www.localiiz.com/post/culture-music-theatre-history-chinese-cantonese-opera.

15. China View TV.Beauty of Kunqu Opera[EB/OL].(2020-01-01)[2022-02-25].https://www.youtube.com/watch?v=3URyBjyJ26Y.

16. China Culture.Introduction of Peking Opera.[EB/OL].(2023-09-07)[2022-02-25].http://en.chinaculture.org/library/2008-01/24/content_44014_2.htm.

17. COLUMBIA UNIVERSITY.CONFUCIAN TEACHING[EB/OL].http://afe.easia.columbia.edu/at/conf_teaching/ct01.html.

18. DANG XIAOFEI. A Summary of Traditional Chinese Festivals[EB/OL].(2019-11-29)[2021-01-10].http://www.chinatoday.com.cn/ctenglish/2018/cs/201911/t20191129_800186428.html.

19. Deng Wei.Magical traditional Chinese medicine: Cupping therapy gains in popularity at home and abroad[EB/OL].(2022-06-13)[2022-12-12].http://en.people.cn/n3/2022/0613/c90000-10109044.html.

20. Hi China.What does the Qingming Festival mean to Chinese people?[Z/OL].(2021-04-04)[2021-01-12].https://www.youtube.com/watch?v=amJjeM8omS4.

21. What is the role of li in Confucianism?[EB/OL].(2020-09-15)[2021-01-10].https://gzipwtf.com/what-is-the-role-of-li-in-confucianism/.

22. Kong Zi[EB/OL].(2020-02-03)[2021-01-10].http://shandong.chinadaily.com.cn/2020-02/03/c_227417.htm.

23. Maggie Hiufu Wong. More than just mooncakes: A guide to Mid-Autumn Festival[EB/OL].(2019-09-13)[2021-01-15]https://edition.cnn.com/travel/article/what-is-mid-autumn-festival/index.html.

24. Mike Ho. Chinese Calendar 2023[EB/OL].(2023-08-14)[2022-04-10]. https://www.chinahighlights.com/travelguide/guidebook/chinese-calendar.htm.

25. Wu Yong. Students say thanks with traditional Laba porridge[EB/OL]. (2021-01-21)[2021-01-15].https://www.chinadaily.com.cn/a/202101/21/WS6008f782a31024ad0baa4277.html.

26. Tania Yeromiyan. What is the Chinese Calendar?[EB/OL].(2022-03-27) [2022-04-10].https://studycli.org/chinese-zodiac/chinese-calendar/.

27. Trish King. Confucius: His Life, Times, and Legacy[EB/OL]. Chattanooga, Tennessee.[2021-01-10].https://www.utc.edu/health-education-and-professional-studies/asia-program/2018-ncta-teaching-modules/confucius.

28. Confucius[EB/OL].(2023-08-27)[2021-03-10].https://en.wikipedia.org/wiki/Confucius.

29. UNFAMILIAR CHINA. Confucian Thought on People[EB/OL].[2021-01-10].https://www.unfamiliarchina.com/all-about-china/confucian-thought-on-people.

30. 李玉良.学而1.1[EB/OL].(2022-01-18)[2022-01-18].https://mp.weixin.qq.com/s/0AcHjBt3jnvLPJhu9XbDgg.

31. Storm Sue.中华传统美德之孝道（英文版）[Z/OL].(2021-03-24)[2022-01-20].https://www.bilibili.com/s/video/BV1F5411N7LD.

32. 想画画的猫.100集向世界介绍中国文化--#5老子 Father of Chinese Philosophy.[Z/OL].(2022-03-13)[2022-03-20].https://www.bilibili.com/video/BV1Gb4y1s7kF?spm_id_from=333.337.search-card.all.click.

33. WILL BUCKINGHAM. Finding Our Way With Laozi.[EB/OL].(2021-03-18)[2021-02-20].https://www.lookingforwisdom.com/laozi/.

34. 可可英语.阴和阳的隐藏含义[Z/OL].(2018-03-07)[2021-02-10].http://

www.kekenet.com/Article/201803/544088.shtml.

35. 胡刀乱剪.让外国人崇拜的【老子】【道家】警世名言.[Z/OL].(2020-04-16)[2021-02-10].https://www.bilibili.com/video/av497753706/.

36. GB TIMES.Traditional Chinese painting | Water, ink and poetry (Hello China #14).[Z/OL].(2012-07-03)[2022-02-10].https://www.youtube.com/watch?v=JNcaXaJv56A.

37. Traditional Chinese painting[EB/OL].[2022-02-10].https://www.shine.cn/Traditional-Chinese-painting/.

38. RUN RUN SHAW LIBRARY. A Quick Introduction to Chinese Painting.[EB/OL].(2010-03-26)[2022-02-10].http://www.cityu.edu.hk/lib/about/event/ch_paint/introduction.htm.

39. New World Encyclopedia. Chinese painting.[EB/OL].(2010-03-26)[2022-02-10].https://www.newworldencyclopedia.org/entry/Chinese_painting.

40. Peter Zhang. Misty Bamboo on a Distant Mountain[EB/OL].(2019-06-14)[2022-02-10].https://www.shine.cn/feature/art-culture/1906144118/.

41. Luo Yan. A Thousand Lis of Rivers and Mountains[EB/OL].(2019-03-10)[2022-02-10].https://www.inkston.com/stories/guides/thousand-lis-rivers-mountains/.

42. Xu Lin. Top 10 most famous Chinese paintings[EB/OL].(2020-06-19)[2022-02-10].http://www.china.org.cn/top10/2011-11/08/content_23854076_10.htm.

43. Alevandro Hintteotti. Beijing Opera[Z/OL].(2015-10-19)[2022-02-25].https://www.youtube.com/watch?v=SQSsL3l_Kac.

44. China Matters. What Is Peking Opera?[EB/OL].(2015-12-04)[2022-02-25].https://www.youtube.com/watch?v=ka5z3uYctug.

45. Nora Zheng. Peking Opera[EB/OL].(2022-12-11)[2022-02-25].https://www.chinaculturetour.com/culture/peking-opera.htm.

46. Top China Travel. Kunqu Opera[EB/OL].https://www.topchinatravel.com/china-guide/kunqu-opera.htm.

47. Ruru Zhou. Chinese Traditional Operas, History of Chinese Opera[EB/OL]. (2021-08-23)[2022-02-25].https://www.chinahighlights.com/travelguide/culture/traditional-operas.htm.

48. 新东方在线.[Z/OL].(2022-05-10)[2022-02-10].https://m.koolearn.com/cet4/20220510/873443.html.

49. Top China Travel. Chinese Handicraft[EB/OL].[2022-02-10].https://www.topchinatravel.com/china-guide/chinese-handicraft/.Gbtimes.Papercutting | An introduction (Hello China #76).[Z/OL].(2012-07-03)[2022-02-10]. https://www.youtube.com/watch?v=gAGjlGsZkx8.

50. Rachel Jiang. Chinese Paper Cutting | Jiǎnzhǐ | Facts, History, Categories & Applications[EB/OL].(2019-04-01)[2022-02-10].https://medium.com/@rachel_82473/chinese-paper-cutting-ji%C7%8Enzh%C7%90-facts-history-categories-applications-191b65a97238.

51. Top China Travel. ChineseKnot[EB/OL].[2022-02-10].https://www.topchinatravel.com/china-guide/chineseknot.htm.

52. China Today. Enchanting Dough Figurines.[EB/OL].(2020-07-25)[2022-02-10].http://www.chinatoday.com.cn/ctenglish/2018/ich/202007/t20200725_800215582.html.

53. Video China TV. China Bouquet EP18 Chasing in the Wind 万象中国 第十八集 引线乘风[Z/OL].(2022-08-17)[2022-12-10].https://www.youtube.com/watch?v=fNSL6rfm8nw.

54. Ji Yuqiao. World Intangible Cultural Heritage[EB/OL].(2020-12-21)[2022-03-10].https://www.globaltimes.cn/content/1210590.shtml.

55．Chinese embroidery[EB/OL].(2023-04-27)[2022-03-10].https://en.wikipedia.org/wiki/Chinese_embroidery.

56. Daniel C. Waugh. Silk[EB/OL].[2022-03-10].https://depts.washington.edu/silkroad/exhibit/trade/silkae.html.

57. Travel China Guide. Chinese Embroidery[EB/OL].(2023-07-05)[2022-03-10]https://www.travelchinaguide.com/intro/arts/embroidery.htm.

58. How beautiful is the high-end cheongsam?You are only one cheongsam away from the style!Noble life and art[EB/OL].(2023-09-07)[2022-03-10] https://inf.news/ne/fashion/d95d2d809549344cbb97df1b777e003b.html.

59. Sally Gao. A Brief History Of The Cheongsam[EB/OL].(2016-12-09)[2022-03-10]https://theculturetrip.com/asia/china/articles/a-brief-history-of-the-cheongsam/.

60. New China TV. Miao embroiderers' new life[EB/OL].(2022-02-22)[2022-03-10].https://www.youtube.com/watch?v=cve2Pflmatk.

61. Janice Damm. A Little History About Chinese Embroidery[EB/OL].(2023-07-04)[2022-03-10].https://www.birdcityfabrics.com/a-little-history-about-chinese-embroidery/.

62. Su Embroidery Studio. The Development of Chinese Embroidery[EB/OL].(2012-10-26)[2022-03-15].http://www.suembroidery.com/embroidery_blog/article/12-10/chinese_embroidery_development.html.

63. Rong Art. CHINESE HANDICRAFT-EMBROIDERY ARTWORKS[EB/OL].(2019-01-04)[2022-03-15].https://www.zeeartsgallery.com/blog/art/chinese-handicraft-embroidery-artwork/.

64. 新东方在线.[Z/OL].(2022-10-13)[2022-02-10].https://m.koolearn.com/cet4/20221013/881705.html.

65. 沈阳新东方.【四级】英语四级翻译练习：旗袍[Z/OL].(2017-08-30)[2022-12-15].http://sy.xdf.cn/cet/201708/308361010.html.

66. 可可英语. 英语四级翻译题模拟：泥塑[Z/OL].(2015-12-03)[2022-03-10].https://m.kekenet.com/cet4/201512/402371.shtml.

67. Catherine He. Chinese Kung Fu (Martial Arts)[EB/OL].(2023-01-02)[2022-03-15].https://www.travelchinaguide.com/intro/martial_arts/.

68. Martial Arts Research & Development Association. Yin Yang Chi Kung Fu[EB/OL].[2022-04-10].https://www.kungfumartialarts.in/yin-yang.php.

69. Ruth Wickham. Chinese Kung Fu[EB/OL].(2023-01-02)[2022-03-15]. https://www.chinaeducationaltours.com/guide/culture-chinese-kungfu.htm.

70. Chinese tea | An introduction (Hello China #74)[Z/OL].(2012-07-03)[2022-05-13].https://www.youtube.com/watch?v=XVMg8JSEEu0.

71. Anne Meredith. Journey into the World of Chinese Tea[EB/OL].(2023-04-29)[2022-05-15].https://studycli.org/chinese-culture/tea/.

72. Topchinatravel. Chinese Tea Culture.[EB/OL].[2022-05-12].https://www.topchinatravel.com/china-guide/chinese-tea-culture/.

73. Asia Pacific. Asian tea culture, explained[EB/OL].(2019-05-17)[2022-05-12].https://news.cgtn.com/news/3d3d514e304d7a4e34457a6333566d54/index.html.

74. Storm Sue. 苏说文化之茶马古道（英文版）[Z/OL].(2021-04-19)[2022-05-12].https://www.bilibili.com/video/BV1A64y1U7xM?share_source=copy_web.

75. Audio news: Chinese tea making joins UNESCO list[Z/OL].(2022-12-07)[2022-12-12].https://enapp.chinadaily.com.cn/a/202212/07/AP63902338a3102cbfe0adc061.html.

76. 英语教学.英文写作：中华茶文化[EB/OL].(2018-05-20)[2022-12-1].https://mp.weixin.qq.com/s/XYJyyLmUpE6uNBCZMw7Kmg.

77. Asian Crush. A Bite of China - OFFICIAL TRAILER - A Culinary and Spiritual Journey Through China[EB/OL].(2014-07-02)[2022-12-1].https://youtu.be/p0BX3HRuYW8.

78. Chinese Food[Z/OL].[2022-06-10].https://www.chinatravel.com/chinese-food.

79. Sally Guo. Chinese Table Manners - 15 Do's and Don'ts[EB/OL].(2023-03-02)[2022-05-12].https://www.chinatravel.com/chinese-food/table-manner.

80. China Discovery. Chinese Dining Etiquette[EB/OL].[2022-05-10].https://www.chinadiscovery.com/chinese-food/dining-etiquette.html.

81. Hi China. Do you really understand chopsticks? | CCTV English[Z/OL].(2018-11-22)[2022-05-15].https://www.youtube.com/watch?v=w-rF1pfXvag.

82. China Travel. 中国八大菜系[Z/OL].(2022-04-26)[2022-05-15].https://www.youtube.com/watch?v=EmVxWKy_pu0.

83. 阿照学习社区.【中国人，中国魂】《Hello China》中国传统文化英文短片全100集（中英双语字幕）[Z/OL].(2021-07-12)[2022-05-15].https://b23.tv/asL0FHm.

84. Anne Meredith. Journey into the World of Chinese Tea[EB/OL].(2023-04-29)[2022-12-3].https://studycli.org/chinese-culture/tea/.

85. Top China Travel. Chinese Tea Culture[EB/OL].[2022-12-3].https://www.topchinatravel.com/china-guide/chinese-tea-culture/.

86. 小赵小赵0v0【新闻剪辑】中国茶文化[Z/OL].(2021-07-15)[2022-12-05].https://www.bilibili.com/video/BV1Ho4y1D7Di?share_source=copy_web.

87. Silk Roads Programme. Dunhuang[EB/OL].(2023-04-29)[2022-12-3].https://en.unesco.org/silkroad/content/dunhuang.

88. VOA慢速英语:壁画艺术为洛杉矶增添色彩[Z/OL].[2022-12-02].https://www.tingclass.net/down-8694-290040-1.html.

89. 2018年12月大学英语四级翻译试题：敦煌莫高窟3篇[EB/OL].(2018-11-30)[2022-12-02].https://www.examw.com/cet4/trans_moni/626139/.

90. Johns Hopkins Medicine. Chinese Medicine[EB/OL].[2022-11-10].https://www.hopkinsmedicine.org/health/wellness-and-prevention/chinese-medicine.

91. Dr. Daniel Chuanxin Wang, DAOM, A.P. Yin-Yang in Traditional Chinese Medicine | Acupuncture and Massage College | Miami, FL[EB/OL].(2019-05-09)[2022-11-10].https://www.amcollege.edu/blog/yin-and-yang-in-traditional-chinese-medicine.

92. 留学生在中国 第13期 Chinese Medicine 中药[EB/OL].(2012-08-27)[2022-11-12].http://www.kekenet.com/menu/201208/196789.shtml.

93. 2015年6月英语四级翻译练习：中医[EB/OL].(2015-02-05)[2022-12-10].https://cet4.koolearn.com/20150205/789899.html.

94. Mayo Clinic Staff. Acupuncture[EB/OL].(2022-04-30)[2022-12-10].https://www.mayoclinic.org/tests-procedures/acupuncture/about/pac-20392763.

95. Nayana Ambardekar, MD. Slideshow: A Visual Guide to Acupuncture[EB/OL].(2022-04-24)[2022-12-10].https://www.webmd.com/pain-management/ss/slideshow-acupuncture-overview.

96. 苗绣：新时代的"绣"色可餐[Z/OL].(2022-06-13)[2022-12-12].https://mp.weixin.qq.com/s/BinHsWd9-R1RXAvxhXwjNQ.

97. 中国驻马德里旅游办事处.Festive China Spring Festival[Z/OL].(2021-01-09)[2021-01-10].https://www.youtube.com/watch?v=LIMBAhpw19Q.

98. 叶丹. 2022高考英语作文押题预[EB/OL].(2022-05-10)[2022-12-15].http://www.gaosan.com/gaokao/371634.html.

99. 林语堂. 老子的智慧[M]. 长沙：湖南文艺出版社. 2016.

100. 王志茹，陆小丽. 英语畅谈中国文化[M]. 北京：外语教学与研究出版社. 2017.

101. 圣才学习网.全国大学生英语竞赛C类、D类真题及模拟试题详解[M]. 北京：中国石化出版社. 2021.

102. 大学英语专业四级、八级历年真题

103. 全国大学英语四级考试真题